OSPREY COMBAT AIRCRAFT • 87

B-24 LIBERATOR
UNITS OF THE CBI

SERIES EDITOR: TONY HOLMES

OSPREY COMBAT AIRCRAFT • 87

B-24 LIBERATOR UNITS OF THE CBI

EDWARD M YOUNG

OSPREY
PUBLISHING

Front Cover
The character of the air war in the China-Burma-India Theatre differed from the European and Mediterranean theatres. The B-24 Liberator bombers of the 7th BG with the Tenth Air Force in India and the 308th BG with the Fourteenth Air Force in China waged a relentless campaign against the Japanese lines of communication. From India, the 7th BG flew many missions targeting the railway system in Burma, while from China the 308th BG concentrated on Japanese shipping, combining low-level attacks on merchant vessels in the China Sea with missions against port facilities along the China coast.

On the morning of 16 October 1944, as part of Mission 278, the 308th BG sent out 28 B-24s to bomb the Kowloon docks in Hong Kong in a combined operation with B-25s from the 341st BG. The B-24s were to bomb the docks from high altitude to draw off the Japanese fighters and flak while the B-25s went in at low level to attack shipping in nearby Victoria harbour. The 308th dropped its bombs at 1340 hrs from an altitude of 17,000 ft, placing 85 per cent of them in the target area as it scored direct hits on the docks and adjacent buildings. The escort of P-51 Mustangs kept the intercepting Japanese fighters at bay. The formation encountered heavy calibre anti-aircraft fire, which the crews described as 'medium intensity, and of fair accuracy'. Most of the flak came after the formation had completed its bomb run. Three aeroplanes received minor damage.

Flying to Hong Kong that day were B-24J-155-CO 44-40316 *Ding How Dottie*, a long-serving veteran of the 373rd BS, and the newly arrived B-24L-1-CO 44-41427 *COCKY BOBBY*, which flew several missions with the 373rd before transferring to the 425th BS (*Cover artwork by Mark Postlethwaite*)

First published in Great Britain in 2011 by Osprey Publishing
Midland House, West Way, Botley, Oxford, OX2 0PH
44-02 23rd St, Suite 219, Long Island City, New York, 11101

E-mail: info@ospreypublishing.com

ISBN: 978 1 84908 341 6
E-book ISBN: 978 1 84908 342 3

Edited by Tony Holmes
Page design by Tony Truscott
Cover Artwork by Mark Postlethwaite
Aircraft Profiles by Mark Styling
Index by Alan Thatcher
Originated by PDQ Digital Media Solutions, Suffolk, UK
Printed in China through Bookbuilders

11 12 13 14 15   10 9 8 7 6 5 4 3 2 1

Osprey Publishing is supporting the Woodland Trust, the UK's leading woodland conservation charity by funding the dedication of trees.

www.ospreypublishing.com

ACKNOWLEDGEMENTS
I would like to extend my sincere thanks to Archie DiFante at the Air Force Historical Research Agency who tracked down the aircraft record cards for the B-24s featured in the colour section of this book. Thank you also to Anthony Strotman for permission to use photographs from the 308th BG and Jim Augustus for permission to use photographs of the 7th BG from his collection. The wonderful staff at the Still Pictures Branch, Archives II, National Archives and Records Service also rendered assistance. Thank you to Dr Mary Ruwell and her staff at the US Air Force Academy Library for permitting me to use photographs from the 7th BG(H) Historical Foundation. Assistance was also given by Dean Stockton and his colleagues who created and maintain the website www.B24BestWeb.com. Thanks also to Brett Stolle at the National Museum of the US Air Force for the use of photographs from the John Osborne collection, the Museum of Flight and my good friend Osamu Tagaya.

CONTENTS

CHINA-BURMA-INDIA

'U.S. Planes Set Fires in Rangoon' ran the headline in *The New York Times*. The April 1942 article reported how American aeroplanes had 'made a smashing night attack on Rangoon', laying down a heavy bombardment on Rangoon's docks, perhaps conjuring in the minds of some readers an image of fleets of mighty four-engined bombers raining bombs down on the Japanese. The reality could not have been more different.

On the night of 3 April 1942, five B-17Es and a single LB-30 (AL608) from the 7th BG took off from Asansol, in India, and flew to Rangoon, where they started three large fires in the dock area with bombs and incendiaries. This was the second combat mission of the newly-formed Tenth Air Force, assigned to the equally new China-Burma-India Theatre, and the first mission over the Asian mainland for the Liberator.

Over the next three-and-a-half years the B-24 Liberator would form the backbone of the two heavy bomber units assigned to the CBI Theatre, the 7th BG of the Tenth Air Force and the 308th BG of the Fourteenth Air Force. Liberators would range over most of China and much of Southeast Asia, bombing from high, medium and low altitudes by day and by night, sweeping the China seas for Japanese shipping, laying mines in the rivers and ports, dive-bombing bridges, strafing locomotives and rolling stock and hauling gasoline and supplies over the dangerous Hump route. Twelve- to fifteen-hour missions would become routine. The B-24's great range, bomb load and versatility made it ideally suited to a theatre of war where terrain, appalling weather, vast distances and inadequate facilities put enormous strains on men and aircraft.

In the early months of 1942, reeling under the successive blows of the Japanese offensive in the Pacific and Southeast Asia, the combined political and military leadership of Britain and the United States, now allies in a global conflict, struggled to adopt a strategy for pursuing the war in the face of rapidly changing circumstances. At the Arcadia Conference at the end of 1941, Prime Minister Winston Churchill and President Franklin Roosevelt, with the combined chiefs of staff, had agreed on the basic outline for Anglo-American strategy. Germany would be the primary enemy and would need to be defeated first. Under the 'Germany First' strategy Europe would be the principal Allied battleground, and would receive priority for supplies and manpower.

Against Japan the Allies agreed to adopt a policy of strategic defence, maintaining the security of the base areas on the flanks of the rapidly expanding Japanese-won territory in Southeast Asia and the Southwest Pacific and protecting the lines of communication to these base areas. Only the minimum forces necessary to safeguard these base areas would be diverted from the attack on Germany. Straightforward in principle, the strategic defence against Japan generated immediate questions as to the exact nature of this defence, how the meagre forces available should be allocated and how to exercise effective control over the units of the several countries involved across a vast geographic area. It soon became apparent that in developing a strategy for the defence of Asia, British and American national interests and strategic objectives were in conflict.

By early February 1942, Allied hopes of slowing the Japanese advance into Southeast Asia were crumbling. The Japanese Army had captured Malaya and was on the verge of capturing Singapore, had pushed deeply into the Dutch East Indies and was on the way to Rangoon, in Burma. The probable loss of Burma posed an immediate threat to India. Not surprisingly, the main interest of the British government was the defence of India and the ultimate re-conquest of its colonies in Southeast Asia. For the United States, the primary objective was to support China.

Since the outbreak of the Sino-Japanese War in August 1937 American sympathies had been with the Chinese people and their desperate struggle against the Japanese. After four years of war, during which time the Chinese armies had suffered more than 1.7 million casualties, China was on the verge of exhaustion, its resources severely depleted and its armed forces poorly trained, poorly equipped and poorly led. The Japanese controlled the coastal areas of China and all the industrial centres, reducing China's ability to receive aid and produce its own war materials.

Before the attack on Pearl Harbor China's only lifeline was the Burma Road, an inadequate route from the port of Rangoon up to the Chinese border at Lashio. China-bound supplies travelled over this one road, including American war materials under Lend-Lease, which had begun in May 1941. With the Japanese conquest of Burma and the loss of the Burma Road, China would be completely cut off from her allies.

For reasons of sentiment and military necessity the United States wanted to ensure that China remained in the war against Japan. There were over a million Japanese troops tied down in China – representing two-fifths of the Japanese Army's divisions – and it was imperative to the defence of the Pacific and India that they remain there. Many in the US military realised that the defeat of Japan would ultimately require attacks on the Japanese homeland, and many, including air power advocates in the USAAC, saw China as the most logical base for such operations.

With the outbreak of war with Japan, sustaining the Chinese war effort by providing immediate and increasing assistance to China became a priority for the United States. By necessity, the base for this effort would have to be India. With the loss of the Burma Road the only supply route to China was the air route from Assam in Northeast India to Kunming in Southwest China, across the Himalaya Mountains, which would become famous as the Hump route. This air route would have to be built up and would need to be defended at both ends against Japanese attack.

To oversee the American effort to support China the War Department created the China-Burma-India Theatre (CBI) and appointed Lt Gen Joseph Stilwell as Theatre Commander. The tasks assigned to Stilwell were onerous. His charge was 'support China', which meant increasing the effectiveness of American assistance to China, building the flow of Lend-Lease supplies and other aid, and improving the efficiency of the

7

Chinese armed forces in order to prosecute the war against Japan. With the loss of Burma, Stilwell concluded that the best way to aid China was to retake Burma and re-open the Burma Road. This objective became the basis for American strategy in the CBI. As long as the Japanese remained in Burma they could threaten the flow of supplies to China.

Churchill and the British Chiefs of Staff thought differently, believing that fighting in the jungles of Burma would negate the Allies' superiority in materiel. They also had a less sanguine view of China's importance to the war against Japan. Far better, they thought, to expand the air route to China and bypass Burma altogether in favour of a seaborne assault on Malaya or Singapore. It would take 18 months for the Allies to agree on a strategy for the war in Burma and to set up a combined command.

7th BG

To assist Stilwell in achieving his objectives the newly activated Tenth Air Force was assigned to the CBI Theatre in February 1942. The Tenth would face challenges unknown to other Army Air Forces. The South Asian Monsoon with strong, often violent winds drenched India and much of Burma with torrential rains from May to September, while the East Asian Monsoon brought similar conditions to Southeast Asia and southern China during the same period of the year. The monsoon season not only obscured targets but made flying through such weather difficult and often dangerous, particularly over the mountain ranges along the border of India and Burma and through the Himalayas. While crews in China had some chance of returning to Allied territory with the help of the Chinese guerrillas, bailing out over Burma meant certain capture.

An inhospitable climate, difficult terrain and a determined foe were bad enough, but the Tenth Air Force and its combat units faced the added difficulties of being at the end of the longest supply line of any American air force and, because of the Germany first strategy, having the lowest priority for aircraft, men and equipment. Compounding the supply problem was the limited industrial base in either India or China necessary to sustain a modern air force and an inadequate transportation system within the theatre. Despite remarkable achievements as the war progressed, logistics would remain an overriding constraint on air operations, especially in China, until the end of the war.

At the end of February Maj Gen Lewis Brereton, who was then serving as the Deputy Commander, Air Forces, ABDACOM (American-British-Dutch-Australian Command) and fighting a desperate battle against the Japanese in Java, was appointed commander of the Tenth Air Force. When Brereton took control on 5 March 1942, the heavy bomber component of his new air force consisted of less than a dozen aircraft – nine B-17Es that had been stopped in India on their way to Java and a single LB-30 that had flown Gen Brereton from Java to India!

These aircraft belonged to the 7th BG, whose units were present at the attack on Pearl Harbor and would fly missions up to war's end. In the autumn of 1941, the 7th BG had three squadrons, the 9th, 11th, and 22nd BSs, and the attached 88th Reconnaissance Squadron (RS), equipped with B-17Es. That November the 7th BG was ordered to the Philippines to reinforce America's air forces. The 88th RS was on its way when it was caught in the Japanese attack on Pearl Harbor.

In the weeks following the attack the group's squadrons made their way to the Pacific, with the 11th BS having exchanged its B-17Es for LB-30s taken from British Lend-Lease contracts. The group was heavily involved in the desperate but futile struggle to halt the Japanese offensive in the Dutch East Indies, and after its withdrawal to Australia in early March 1942 Gen Brereton ordered the remnants of the group to transfer to India, where it began flying missions against the Japanese in Burma using the few B-17Es available to the 9th BS.

Brereton initially planned to reorganise the 7th as a composite group, with two heavy and two medium bomber squadrons, but before this could be fully implemented Rommel's advance into Egypt in June 1942 caused Brereton's transfer to the Middle East together with the 9th BS and all available heavy bombers in India. This move left the 7th BG with just one heavy bomber squadron, the 436th BS (as the 88th RS had been re-designated), and two squadrons, the 11th and 22nd BSs, now flying B-25 medium bombers. The 436th and 22nd BSs were scattered across India, with crews and aircraft dribbling in from the US, while the 11th BS had been transferred to China to join the China Air Task Force (CATF) under Brig Gen Claire Chennault, which had been organised under the Tenth Air Force to control American air units in China.

That same month Gen Hap Arnold and Air Chief Marshal Sir Charles Portal agreed on the size and composition of USAAF units that would serve in Asia. Under this plan the Tenth Air Force would have one heavy bomber group, one medium bomber group and two fighter groups. Brig Gen Clayton Bissell, who took over command of the Tenth in August 1942, oversaw the conversion of the 7th BG back to a heavy bomber group of four squadrons. The latter were the 9th BS, which was still in the Middle East, the 436th BS and two new squadrons activated in the theatre, the 492nd and 493rd BSs, all under the command of Col Conrad F Necrason, who had led the 9th BS in Java.

The 11th and 22nd BSs were transferred to the new 341st BG (Medium). Bissell did not consider the B-17 suitable for the CBI Theatre because of its relative lack of range. He wrote to Gen Arnold requesting that the 7th BG be re-equipped with the B-24 Liberator. Arnold agreed, but because of the demands of other theatres it would be some months before the 7th BG received its full complement of aircraft.

INDIA AIR TASK FORCE

To control and coordinate American air units in India, Brig Gen Bissell activated the India Air Task Force (IATF) on 3 October 1942 under Col Caleb Haynes. The IATF's mission was to defend USAAF air bases in Assam and to prevent any further Japanese advance. One means of achieving this goal was to weaken the Japanese Army's air and ground forces in Burma through air attack.

The Japanese Army had its own logistical problems to contend with. While Burma could provide much of the Army's need for food and

A USAAF B-24D is seen at the RAF air depot at Karachi on its way to the 7th BG in India in 1942. The aircraft parked behind it is an RAF Liberator II (*Peter Bowers Collection, Museum of Flight*)

clothing, all military equipment and supplies had to come from Japan over a 4000-mile line of communications, travelling by boat through the East and South China seas to ports in Burma or nearby Thailand or Singapore, and then by rail up into the interior of Burma to the frontlines. The rail system consisted of some 2000 miles of single track lines from Thailand and Malaya to Rangoon, then north through the central Burmese plain up to Mandalay and Myitkyina.

This entire system of transportation was vulnerable to attack and disruption, with a wealth of potential targets in port and dock facilities, warehouses, marshalling yards, rail centres and vital bridges along the route. With few industrial targets of any worth, the air war in Burma became a war against enemy communications and supplies. With its longer range, the B-24 gave the Tenth Air Force a wider choice of targets.

The objectives and targets Col Haynes selected for his two bomber groups set the pattern of attacks for much of the rest of the war. The interruption of the movement and transshipment of supplies by sea or land into lower Burma became the primary objective of the 7th BG with its long-range Liberators. Disrupting the movement of supplies from lower Burma to the frontlines was the responsibility of both the 7th BG and the medium bombers of the 341st BG, with the Mitchells covering targets within their range in central Burma. In these missions the Tenth Air Force loosely cooperated with the Royal Air Force in India. Real coordination did not come about until a year later.

The 7th BG's first mission with its new Liberator bombers, however, was to China. In early October 1942 five new B-24Ds arrived in India from the US for a special mission. Maj Max Fennell, who had made several flights into China earlier in the year, flew out from the Middle East in his own B-24 to command the mission. The target was the Lin-Hsi coal mines in northern China east of Peking (Beijing), which was a major source of coking coal for the Japanese steel industry.

Drawing crews from the 436th BS, Fennell led six B-24s to the airfield at Chengtu, north of Chungking. On the morning of 21 October, they took off in clear weather and flew north without encountering any opposition. One aircraft had to abort just before reaching the target, but the remaining five bombed individually from 14,000 ft. Their ordnance did considerable damage to the mine installations but failed to destroy the vital power plant and pumping stations. The bombers returned to the 436th BS's base at Allahabad, northwest of Calcutta.

With the arrival of a few more new B-24Ds, the 436th began flying missions into Burma. On 27 October, four aircraft were sent to bomb Lashio on the China-Burma border. On the night of 29/30 October, the

One of the crews that flew to China to bomb the Lin-Hsi coal mines on 21 October 1942 pose with local troops at Chengtu after the mission (*7th BG(H) Historical Foundation, USAFA McDermott Library*)

7th BG experienced its first aircraft loss. The 436th sent ten aeroplanes to bomb Rangoon. Poor weather prevented the aeroplane of Lt William Berkeley from reaching the target. While over the Bay of Bengal on the flight back to base, a fire broke out in the nose of the aircraft and then all four electric generators burned out, leaving the B-24 without any electrical systems. Berkeley flew on with his co-pilot shining a torch on the instrument panel. Approaching Calcutta, the engines began to run away. Berkeley ordered the crew to bail out, which they did successfully.

A week later on 5 November, the 436th sent seven B-24s back to Rangoon on a daylight raid to bomb the dock areas along the Rangoon River. The high altitude attack at midday caught the Japanese by surprise. Returning crews reported hits on warehouses and a small ship in the harbour, with only weak flak over the target area. Returning to Rangoon for another daytime raid four days later, six B-24s from the 436th found a warmer reception. The harbour area and nearby warehouses were again the target, but this time the bombers had to fly through heavier and more accurate anti-aircraft fire and encountered Japanese Army Air Force (JAAF) fighters for the first time. Three of the latter flew near the formation and one attempted to make an attacking pass, but it was driven off by the rear gunners' fire.

It took time for the 7th BG to build up to its full strength. At the end of the first week of November the 436th BS received its 12th B-24D, and shortly thereafter moved station to Gaya, an airfield 150 miles closer to Calcutta. The 9th BS, transferred back to India from the Middle East, joined the 436th BS at Gaya, having stopped at Karachi to pick up several new B-24Ds. The group's 492nd and 493rd BSs were still in cadre status at Karachi, awaiting crews and aircraft.

On 20 November Col Necrason led nine aircraft from the 436th BS to bomb the marshalling yards at Mandalay. In clear weather the eight aircraft that reached the target caught up to 700 units of rolling stock in the yards and dropped 40 1000-lb bombs on the yards and nearby repair workshops. Two days later the 9th BS borrowed three aircraft from the 436th, and with three of its own B-24s returned to the same target, scoring a direct hit on the repair shop.

Then on the night of 25 November, Necrason led three aircraft from the 9th BS and six from the 436th BS on what was the longest bombing mission of the war to date – a 2760-mile round trip to attack an oil refinery and powerplant in Bangkok, Thailand. The aeroplanes took off at three-minute intervals. A 436th BS B-24 had to abort when its undercarriage failed to retract, but the rest continued on to the target, bombing individually from 12,000 ft up, with 200-ft spacing between aircraft. Four nights later, the 436th BS sent out six B-24s on a mission to bomb the docks at Rangoon. The aeroplanes departed Gaya at 2200 hrs at five-minute intervals. Once over the target the bombers encountered searchlights and heavy anti-aircraft fire. The Liberator flown by Lt Thomas Ackerman failed to return, having possibly fallen victim to flak.

For the next month the IATF had the 7th BG concentrate its effort on restricting the movement of shipping across the Gulf of Martaban into Rangoon. There were two raids on shipping in the Andaman Islands, the 9th BS attacking Port Blair on 30 November (one aircraft from the

436th BS claimed a naval auxiliary ship hit) and the 436th BS returning to this target on 11 December with six aircraft. The latter mission lasted more than 12 hours, and results were mixed due to poor weather.

The majority of the month's missions were to the Rangoon docks, with the 9th BS attacking this target on 7 and 11 December. During the latter operation a B-24 and its crew were borrowed from the 436th BS, which flew the next mission to Rangoon on 20 December. First off at 0600 hrs was a flight of three aircraft sent to bomb the JAAF airfield at Mingaladon. The main flight of six aircraft departed 45 minutes later, hitting the docks. The 9th BS returned to Rangoon the following day.

Then, on the last mission of the year on 29 December, a flight of six aircraft from the 9th BS and five from the 436th BS went after shipping near Rangoon. One flight attacked a 5000-ton tanker heading from Moulmein to Rangoon, leaving it in flames, while the other flight found a large freighter of 5000 to 6000 tons in the mouth of the Rangoon River, damaging it so that the ship came to a complete stop. In between the two Rangoon missions the 9th sent 12 aircraft on the second night raid on Bangkok. Three B-24s attacked the dock area on the Chao Phya River, three bombed the main railway station and six aircraft targeted the Bangkok arsenal, returning to Pandaveswar after 14 hours in the air.

None of the daylight raids to Rangoon encountered any opposition. At the time the two Japanese fighter units in Burma, the 50th and 64th Sentais, were based in the north to counter the RAF along the India-Burma border and to support attacks on American air bases in Assam.

During December the 7th BG headquarters and the 9th BS moved to a new base at Pandaveswar, nicknamed 'Panda', which was near the town of Asansol in Bengal Province northwest of Calcutta. Here they were joined by the cadre of the 493rd BS. The 436th BS remained at Gaya and took on the cadre of the 492nd BS which, like the 493rd, was still awaiting both crews and aircraft.

Gen Arnold had planned that the Tenth Air Force's heavy bomber group would have 35 B-24s by October 1942. At year end the 7th BG could only muster 32 bombers, and ten of these were older B-17 Flying Fortresses that were considered to be non-operational. Despite the shortage of crews and aircraft, in more than a dozen missions the Liberators had proven their worth, striking regularly at Rangoon and making the first heavy bomber raids to Bangkok with the loss of only one aircraft.

With the RAF hitting targets in Burma by night and the Tenth Air Force by day, the Japanese could only guess that heavier raids would be likely during the coming year, bringing further disruption to the flow of supplies to the front. A more active defence of Rangoon was clearly necessary.

Lts Tom Murphy, William Berkeley and Richard Weiss pose near an early B-24D from the 436th BS at Gaya, in India, in late 1942 (*7th BG(H) Historical Foundation, USAFA McDermott Library*)

OPERATIONS DURING 1943

In the New Year rail centres and bridges were added to merchant shipping and dock facilities as priority strategic targets for the 7th BG. For its first mission of 1943, on 4 January the group sent six Liberators from the 436th BS and four from the 9th BS to bomb the rail yards at Mandalay, where the bombers again found a concentration of rolling stock. The bombing set off fires, with smoke columns that could still be seen when the bombers were 70 miles away. RAF Wellington bombers followed up with a night attack.

That same day the 9th BS sent three B-24s on a shipping sweep south of Rangoon, where the bombers caught a 15,000-ton transport moving up the Rangoon River. They scored two direct hits and three near misses with 500-lb bombs, leaving the vessel smoking. On the way back to base the flight bombed the Rangoon docks, where two Japanese fighters intercepted the formation without result.

The 9th BS sent six B-24s out on a shipping sweep again on 15 January, which located a Japanese convoy of two freighters and a sub-chaser in the Gulf of Martaban. The six aeroplanes made individual runs on the two freighters, sinking one ship with 500-lb bombs and leaving the other smoking. Meanwhile, the 436th BS had begun what would become a long-running battle between the perseverance of the 7th BG's B-24s and the ingenuity and determination of Japanese repair crews.

On 10 January six B-24s from the 436th BS, joined by two flights of eight B-25s from the 22nd and 491st BSs, bombed the Myitnge Bridge – a vital railway bridge south of Mandalay. The Liberators went in at 15,000 ft, dropping 27 500-lb and 15 1000-lb bombs. Three of the latter weapons downed one of the bridge spans into the Myitnge River. As a follow-up to the raids on the Mandalay railway yards and the Myitnge Bridge, a flight of four B-24s from the 9th BS bombed the railway junction at Thazi, 80 miles south of Mandalay, on 19 January.

This series of raids on shipping and rail communications illustrate how the Tenth Air Force's strategy worked in practice. The shipping sweeps disrupted the flow of supplies into Rangoon while the raids on the railway system compounded the Japanese logistical problem by delaying the flow of supplies to the north over the Burmese rail network. Evidence that these raids were having an effect,

A 9th BS B-24D flies over India in early 1943. At this time the 7th BG painted out the serial numbers on many of its bombers, leaving only a two-numeral aeroplane number visible on the fins (*Peter M Bowers Collection, Museum of Flight*)

despite the small number of aeroplanes employed, came from a daring daylight reconnaissance mission into Thailand when Col Necrason took three B-24s from the 9th BS to Kanchanaburi, 75 miles northwest of Bangkok. Here, they photographed the construction of a new railway line from Thailand to Burma, indicating that the Japanese were clearly anticipating that the flow of ships to Rangoon would be cut off. Returning to Pandaveswar from this mission, Lt J R Barton found when he lowered his landing gear that one of the main tyres was flat. He calmly instructed one of his gunners to shoot out the other tyre and landed without incident.

The 7th BG had its first serious fight with Japanese fighters on the debut mission for the 493rd BS. With an influx of crews and aeroplanes, both the 492nd and the 493rd BSs became operational during January. The 492nd, which adopted the name 'The Eager Beaver Bombing Company', flew its first mission on 24 January, sending nine aircraft to bomb the Rangoon docks without incident.

Two days later the 493rd BS sortied seven B-24s to join seven from the 9th BS on a mission to the same target. Approaching the docks at 21,000 ft, the formation encountered heavy anti-aircraft fire, but crews put most of their bombs in the target area. Leaving Rangoon, the Liberators ran into six Ki-43-II 'Oscar' fighters from the 50th Sentai, which had scrambled and climbed to the bombers' altitude. Charles Duncan, a co-pilot in the 9th BS on the mission, later wrote;

'The agile little aeroplanes would fly parallel to our formation, usually out of range to our right. After pulling well ahead of us, and gaining a slight altitude advantage, they would wheel and come boring in from near head-on. When they came within range from this "11 o'clock" to "1 o'clock" position, little winking red lights showed up on the top of the engine cowling. Just when it appeared inevitable that there must be a mid-air collision, they would snap over on their backs and dive down and away from our formation. They would disappear for a while, but soon reappear, climbing to our right to repeat the process.'

The B-24s' defensive fire damaged all six 'Oscars', whose pilots had claimed four Liberators shot down – none were lost in the encounter.

A B-24D taxies in at Pandaveswar, in India, after a mission in 1943. Note the aircraft's bomb tally below the cockpit, as well as the silhouette of a sinking ship to denote that it had successfully destroyed a Japanese vessel (*3A-33641, RG342FH, NARA*)

7th BG crews prepare for a mission at Pandaveswar in February 1943 (*3A-34837, RG342FH, NARA*)

The Japanese fighter pilots were finding that with only two 12.7 mm machine guns fitted to their Ki-43-IIs, the B-24 took some considerable effort to shoot down, but this would not deter them from trying.

With a few more aircraft available, the 7th BG could increase the frequency of missions over Burma and the number of aircraft sent out on each mission, although the 492nd and 493rd BSs occasionally had to borrow bombers from their sister squadrons to make up the numbers. During February the group continued to hammer at targets in and around Rangoon that supported the flow of supplies to the front, bombing the dock areas along the Rangoon River, the nearby warehouses, the Mahlwagon marshalling yards, the Rangoon railway station and the important Pazundaung Bridge. The latter was a 500 ft-long bridge crossing over a tributary of the Rangoon River that carried the railway line to the north. In an effort to hamper Japanese fighter defences around Rangoon, Mingaladon airfield – the main JAAF fighter base in the area – also became a frequent target.

The 9th BS began the month's strikes on Rangoon with a mission by seven aircraft to bomb both the docks and shipping in the Rangoon River on 1 February. One week later on the 8th, in the largest B-24 mission to date, the 7th BG sent 19 aircraft from the 436th, 492nd and the

Lt David Kellogg pilots his B-24D on a mission during 1943. Kellogg would subsequently rise through the ranks to command the 9th BS (*7th BG(H) Historical Foundation, USAFA McDermott Library*)

493rd BSs to target the Mahlwagon marshalling yards and the dock area, while another three aircraft from the 492nd BS bombed the runway at Mingaladon.

Coming off the target, the 436th BS formation ran into six Ki-43-IIs. The 'Oscar' pilots made repeated attacks over the next 30 minutes, concentrating their fire on the second element in the formation. The aeroplane flown by Lt German was riddled, his radio operator being killed and two of his gunners badly wounded. The B-24 gunners claimed one 'Oscar' destroyed and two more probably destroyed, but none appear to have been lost.

Four days later the 436th sent seven aircraft to bomb the Mahlwagon marshalling yards, while six aircraft from the 492nd bombed the dock areas, all without opposition. The final attack on the Rangoon area came on the last day of the month when the 9th and 436th BSs sent 11 aircraft to attack the Pazundaung rail bridge.

While trying to disrupt the flow of supplies into Rangoon, the 7th BG continued to restrict the movement of war materiel north to the front, flying five missions during the month against the key Myitnge Bridge. On 12 February the 493rd BS employed 2000-lb bombs for the first time, followed three days later by the 9th BS, which dropped 11 of them on the bridge. However, even when flying at medium altitudes (15,000-17,000 ft) in clear weather and with minimal anti-aircraft fire, a bridge with a width of just 12 ft to 20 ft proved to be an exceedingly difficult target to hit. Indeed, the ratio of hits to misses proved frustratingly high. Often, the best that could be achieved was damage to the approaches to the bridge, which could be quickly repaired, requiring another mission to bomb the bridge again just days later.

At the end of February the 7th BG began a campaign of mining enemy harbours that would continue through to war's end. The Tenth Air Force wanted to mine the Rangoon harbour area and the estuaries of the Rangoon and Irrawaddy Rivers as part of the objective to restrict the flow of supplies into the city. The initial experiment was designated Project *Low*. Lacking US-made magnetic mines, the Tenth turned to the RAF for assistance. The latter arranged for the Royal Navy to give the Tenth 300 British Type A Mk V 1000-lb magnetic mines, and with technical support from the RAF these were modified to fit within the bomb-bay of the B-24. The Liberator could accommodate four mines, but at the expense of the bomb-bay fuel tanks which restricted the aircraft's range.

On the night of 22 February 11 B-24s from the 492nd and 493rd BSs, with several RAF Liberator IIs, flew down the Bay of Bengal and into the Gulf of Martaban to head north up the river estuaries, descending to 500 ft under low cloud. The mines had to be laid with precision in a specific pattern to be most effective. As a diversion, six aircraft from the 436th BS carried out raids on the Mahlwagon marshalling yards and Mingaladon airfield. One of the mine-laying bombers failed to find its target area, but the rest laid 40 mines accurately. Photographic reconnaissance noted that no shipping passed through Rangoon for the next several weeks. For the rest of the year the 7th BG conducted mining missions in and around Rangoon every four to six weeks, switching to the American Mk 13 aerial mine during the summer of 1943.

So far the 7th BG's B-24s had been able to range over Burma with relative impunity. The 7th BG was fortunate in that the bulk of the 50th and 64th Sentais were pre-occupied at the time with supporting the Japanese Army's counterattacks against the British in the Akyab area far from Rangoon. Small bomber formations had therefore managed to attack targets in the city without interception. The few encounters with Japanese fighters had been inconclusive. This good fortune was not to last, as JAAF pilots quickly learned that the best way to attack a B-24 was from the less well-defended front quarter, with repeated close passes

Arrows Represent Bomb Bursts

This photograph was taken during an attack on the docks at Bassein on 8 March 1943. Images such as this were analysed post-mission to determine the effectiveness of the Liberators' bombing (*3A-37507, RG342FH, NARA*)

being made in an attempt to knock out an engine or incapacitate the pilot and co-pilot. March would bring the Japanese their first successes as they responded more aggressively to the B-24 raids.

On 10 March four bombers from the 492nd BS that were sent to bomb Mingaladon airfield ran into some 14 fighters. In the running battle that ensued, the B-24 gunners claimed three 'Oscars' destroyed, four probables and four damaged, although it does not appear that any Japanese fighters were in fact lost that day.

During the month the 7th BG made a concerted effort to knock out the Pazundaung Bridge in Rangoon, sending out small flights of four to six aircraft on eight separate occasions against this important rail bridge. On 12 March the 436th BS sent six aircraft to bomb the bridge. Four or five Ki-43-IIs attacked the formation, as did four twin-engined Ki-45 'Nick' fighters from the recently arrived 21st Sentai in their first encounter with the B-24s. The bombers claimed an 'Oscar' and a 'Nick' shot down, although again none seem to have been lost. The next day the 9th BS sent out four aircraft on the unit's third mission to the bridge, each B-24 being armed with five 1000-lb bombs.

Three days earlier, on 10 March, the squadron had run into a single fighter which attacked without result, but after the bomb run the unit was intercepted by at least seven fighters, possibly from the 50th Sentai. In a persistent attack the fighters inflicted fatal damage to the aircraft flown by Capt James Baldwin and Lt Willard Short. Both B-24s crashed in the Gulf of Martaban south of Rangoon, killing all on board.

On 18 March the 9th and 436th BSs conducted a joint attack on the Pazundaung Bridge with ten aircraft. Four Ki-45s from the 21st Sentai attacked the formation, with the bombers claiming one 'Nick' damaged. The next encounter took place on the last day of the month, when Col Necrason, flying with the 493rd BS, led 22 aircraft from all four 7th BG squadrons against the rail bridge and marshalling yards at Pyinmana on the line north to Mandalay.

En route to the target the formation happened to run into a flight of 13 Ki-43-IIs from the 64th Sentai led by ace Capt Yasuhiko Kuroe, commander of the 3rd Chutai. The fighters, on their way to Chittagong, attacked immediately, Kuroe and his wingman targeting a B-24 from the rear despite hits from the bombers' return fire. Other Japanese pilots saw the bomber go down. This appears to have been the aeroplane of Lt Lloyd Jensen of the 9th BS, which was forced out of the formation and subsequently crashed. Jensen, his co-pilot and two of his gunners bailed out successfully to become PoWs, but the rest of the crew were killed. The other Japanese fighters made a repeated series of well-coordinated attacks on the formation, the fight lasting for 50 minutes.

As the second element of the 493rd BS began its bomb run, three 'Oscars' attacked from above at '10 o'clock', while another three launched a simultaneous pass from the '2 o'clock' position, crossing over the second element at the end of their firing passes. Shortly thereafter a single Ki-43-II made a determined attack on the lead ship of the element that Col Necrason was flying. An explosive shell went through the centre panel of the front windscreen, the fragments wounding Necrason in his shoulder and his co-pilot in the neck. The 9th BS, which apparently faced the brunt of the attacks, claimed two fighters destroyed and hits on five others, which was not far off the mark. Four 'Oscars' had to force-land after the combat and several more were damaged.

During April the bombers held their own against the JAAF fighters. The 7th BG flew missions by day and by night to familiar targets in the Rangoon area, sending out units singly or in pairs. As most of the day missions started with a morning take-off and a four- to five-hour flight to the target, the 9th BS later formed the 'Goon at Noon' Club, open to all who had completed an unescorted mission over the city at that hour.

The bombers sought out other targets in Burma, bombing a Japanese headquarters in Toungoo, as well as the town of Prome and the jetty area in Bassein, south of Moulmein on the Gulf of Martaban, during the first half of the month. On a mission to bomb the Mahlwagon marshalling yards in Rangoon on 6 April, the 492nd BS ran into a flight of 'Oscars' but these were driven off, with the gunners claiming one as probably destroyed.

In mid-April the 7th BG arranged for three P-40 fighters from the 51st FG to be sent on detached service with the group. For the next several weeks the Warhawks exercised with the group's squadrons, giving the gunners practice in tracking fighter approaches. This training paid off during the rest of the month.

The 493rd FS sent six aircraft to bomb the Pazundaung Bridge on 17 April, making two runs on this difficult target and scoring several near misses. After the second bomb run, two 'Oscars' and an unidentified third fighter with an in-line engine and an air scoop under the fuselage (which fits a description of the Kawasaki Ki-61 Hien, several examples of which had been assigned to the 50th Sentai as possible replacements for the Ki-43-II) launched head-on attacks on the first element. Concentrating their fire on the element leader, they pressed home their attacks to within 20 ft of the B-24s. The bombers responded with a terrific burst of fire. The 'Oscars' repeated their attacks twice more, without result.

After flying three night missions, two to the rail yards in Rangoon and one a return attack on the main railway station in Bangkok, as well as a nearby arsenal, the 436th and 493rd BSs sent 17 aircraft to bomb the Thilwa oil refinery near Rangoon on 26 April. After the bomb run four Ki-45 fighters attacked the 493rd's formation,

A formation of B-24Ds on the way to Rangoon during 1943. For most of the year the 7th BG flew these long-range missions without fighter escort (3A-33602, RG342FH, NARA)

B-24D *We're Wolves* crashed on take-off when departing on a mission from Pandaveswar in May 1943, the aircraft spewing bombs out of its bomb-bay as it careered off the runway. Fortunately, their fusing pins were still firmly in place at the time (*7th BG(H) Historical Foundation, USAFA McDermott Library*)

concentrating on the No 2 aeroplane in the first element as it had lost an engine to anti-aircraft fire. The 'Nicks' made individual attacks from the '11 o'clock' and '1 o'clock' positions, raking the B-24 formation and then flying over it. In a battle that lasted 40 minutes, the gunners saw a Ki-45 break off smoking badly. Despite their heavier armament (two 12.7 mm machine guns and one 20 mm or 37 mm cannon), the 'Nicks' did remarkably little damage to the B-24s.

With the monsoon season approaching, the 7th BG launched a flurry of missions during May against targets all over Burma, hitting railway yards, storage areas and Japanese Army barracks. Almost all of these missions were flown by individual squadrons, each unit typically sending out six to nine aircraft per mission. Each of the group's four squadrons flew nearly double the number of sorties flown in April, collectively dropping the highest tonnage of bombs for the entire year. A number of missions were to targets in central Burma to support the efforts of the medium bombers.

The month began with a group mission to bomb shipping in and around Rangoon on 1 May. The 492nd BS ran into a group of 'Oscars' from the 2nd Chutai of the 64th Sentai after their bomb run. In a frontal attack ace Sgt Miyoshi Watanabe knocked out two engines on Lt Robert Kavanagh's bomber and then attacked from the rear, ramming the rear turret and then bailing out of his damaged fighter. Kavanagh dived for the ground calling for help. The squadron leader, Capt Delahay, dove the entire 492nd BS formation down to 2500 ft in an attempt to provide cover for Kavanagh's stricken aeroplane, which was still under attack. Kavanagh could not keep up with the rest of the flight, however, and Lt Hirao Yukimoto and WO Takamoto administered the coup de grace, Kavanagh's aeroplane finally crash-landing in a rice paddy, two of the crew having been killed in the fight. The rest were taken prisoner.

The group had a modicum of revenge a week later when the 9th and 493rd BSs were sent to bomb the railway yards at Toungoo. After

This photograph, published in the December 1943 issue of the Japanese aviation magazine *Koku Asahi*, shows Lt Robert Kavanagh's B-24D after it was shot down on 1 May 1943 while attacking shipping in Rangoon harbour (*Author's Collection*)

With its bomb-bay doors open, the 493rd BS's B-24D-10-CO 41-23921 *"Sittin' Bull"* approaches the docks at Rangoon during a September 1943 mission (*3A-33755, RG342FH, NARA*)

The crew of *Sittin' Bull* after completing their 50th mission (*3A-34795, RG342FH, NARA*)

successfully dropping their bombs in the target area, the formation turned for home, the gunners calling out that three enemy fighters were climbing up from below. Three Ki-43s intercepted the formation five minutes later, launching attacks from the front quarter. In a change of tactics the Japanese fighters came in at nose level or slightly below to avoid the fire from the B-24's top turret. In repeated attacks which lasted 40 minutes, five of six B-24s in the 493rd BS formation were hit and two crewmen wounded. One of the 'Oscars' was shot down, the wing being seen to break off and the pilot bail out. A second Ki-43-II dived away smoking badly.

On 11 May the 493rd again ran into an element of 'Oscars' on a mission to the Syriam Oil Refinery near Rangoon. The JAAF fighters attacked after the bomb run, which left the refinery area burning with large fires. Three

Renamed *RANGOON RAMBLER*, *"Sittin' Bull"* was sent back to the United States with a tour-expired scratch crew for a bond tour. Maj Gen George Stratemeyer stands with the lucky few heading back to 'Paradise', as many crews called home (*3A-34796, RG342FH, NARA*)

DESTINY'S TOT, a 9th BS B-24D, racks up yet another bombing mission in 1943 (*3A-34970, RG342FH, NARA*)

Ki-43-IIs made head-on attacks, although none were pressed home with the determination of previous encounters. One aircraft was seen to be descending rapidly after the encounter. This may have been the aeroplane of Lt Hirao Yukimoto of the 64th Sentai, which burst into flames when its pilot attempted an emergency landing after it had been hit during an attack on the B-24 formation.

Towards the end of May the monsoon started. For the next few months until the end of September the weather would play havoc with bombing missions. The 7th BG continued to fly as often as it could, but numerous sorties had to be abandoned due to adverse weather. The squadrons again conducted many individual missions, sending out small formations of bombers. The bombers would plough through wide bands of cloud encountering torrential rain and severe turbulence, only to find that the target was covered over in ten-tenths cloud. The group started directing the squadrons to targets in central Burma, which was somewhat drier and less affected by the monsoon rains, if the primary target was covered in cloud. The small formations proved better able to handle the weaving around cloud formations to find an approach to the target.

The weather had a similar impact on Japanese fighter operations. There were few interceptions, although on a 2 July mission the 493rd ran into an exceptionally determined Ki-45 pilot in what the squadron reported as 'another exciting adventure'. Despite intense return fire, the solitary 'Nick' made six passes against the formation of six bombers, the pilot showing 'unusual daring and skill'. Indeed, he even allowed his rear gunner to bring his gun into action. Incredibly only one bomber was hit in the encounter.

On 6 September all four squadrons went on a mission to bomb shipping in Rangoon harbour, each squadron attacking separately. The 9th and 492nd BSs ran into five Ki-45 s and three Ki-43-IIs, and in the ensuing combat claimed one 'Nick' and one 'Oscar' destroyed and two Ki-45s and a Ki-43-II as probables. The 64th Sentai lost ace Lt Shunji Takahashi, one of its leading pilots.

The monsoon weather lasted until the end of September. In the remaining months of the year the 7th BG would initiate a change in tactics with newer aircraft and engage in the most intense and bitter combat yet encountered.

AIR BATTLES OVER RANGOON

With the weather clearing, regular missions resumed in October. There had been several command changes during the monsoon season which would affect the 7th BG. In July Brig Gen Howard Davidson replaced Brig Gen Clayton Bissell as commander of the Tenth Air Force, while in

In October 1943 the 7th BG began replacing its older B-24Ds with newer J-models. *Strawberry Queen*, shown here undergoing maintenance, was one of the B-24Js that joined the group that autumn (*7th BG(H) Historical Foundation, USAFA McDermott Library*)

August Maj Gen George Stratemeyer arrived to take up the new position of Commander, HQ USAAF India-Burma Sector, CBI Theatre.

During the month new B-24Js arrived to replace the older D-models. Opinions on the new aeroplanes were mixed, for while appreciating the heavier armament in the nose and belly turrets, pilots found the J-model to be slower, heavier and less manoeuvrable than the D, and some parted with their older aircraft reluctantly. By the end of the month all four squadrons had nearly a full complement of B-24Js.

In a change of tactics the 7th BG began flying more group missions involving all four squadrons. There were fewer individual squadron missions, and when not flying on a group mission the units more often went out in pairs partly to inflict greater damage on their targets and partly to defend against a much more aggressive Japanese fighter force. As the 436th BS recorded in its squadron history for October 1943, 'the Japs seemed to be very eager. They pressed their attacks home in a whole-hearted manner and seemed to be very interested in grabbing some glory'.

The JAAF had decided to send reinforcements to Burma to support the 50th and 64th Sentais. During October the 33rd Sentai began arriving at bases in southern and northern Burma, while in November the 204th Sentai was sent to Mingaladon to beef up the fighter defences around Rangoon. Newer aircraft arrived in the form of eight Nakajima Ki-44 Shoki ('Tojo') fighters, which were divided between the 50th and the 64th. During the monsoon the 64th had withdrawn to Singapore where the pilots had undertaken practice attacks on a captured B-17 to refine their tactics against the B-24s. The Japanese pilots were eager and their attacks on the B-24 formations more frequent, more determined and, unfortunately for the 7th BG, more damaging.

After several squadron sea sweeps on 1 October, the 7th BG sent 26 aircraft to bomb shipping near Rangoon on the 3rd and 27 to the same targets the very next day. Japanese fighters intercepted both raids, but in repeated attacks failed to inflict any damage. The 9th BS claimed two destroyed and one probable on the mission of 3 October and two more destroyed the following day. For the next week the bombers attacked targets in other areas of Burma, concentrating on railway yards and inflicting severe damage at Pyinmana and Sagaing.

On 14 October, the group sent 28 aircraft from the 9th, 436th and 493rd BSs to bomb shipping at Rangoon and the dock areas. However, instead of striking these targets, the 436th broke away from the main formation and bombed the Prome railway yards instead. The 9th and 493rd continued on to Rangoon, where they attacked their secondary targets – a foundry and motor works. Seven Ki-45s and nine Ki-43-IIs attacked the bombers just as they released their bombs, the JAAF fighters harassing the Liberators for more than an hour.

In one of the many passes the Japanese aircraft made against the 493rd's formation, the B-24D of Lt Harold Goad was hit in the bomb-bay fuel tank, which immediately caught fire. Aeroplanes flying nearby saw a crewman desperately hacking away at the straps holding the tank in place, and it was seen to fall away. Goad's aeroplane had been fatally damaged however, for a few minutes later the left wing broke off and the aeroplane began to disintegrate. Five of the crew managed to bail out to become PoWs.

Four days later the 9th and 493rd BSs paired up to attack the Japanese airfield at Heho. The bombers made two runs on the target, and shortly afterwards five Ki-43-IIs attacked, concentrating on the 9th's formation. Lt William McHenry's aircraft was hit hard and dropped out of formation, the 'Oscars' zooming in on the crippled bomber. After one pass the left wing was seen to come off and the bomber spiralled down into the clouds below. Six of the crew managed to bail out. Two other bombers were moderately damaged, one force-landing at the RAF airfield at Chittagong. The bombers claimed one fighter destroyed and one probable, but none were lost.

The next encounter took place on 26 October, and this time it was the 492nd's turn to suffer a loss. The 7th BG sent out 28 aircraft to target shipping in Rangoon, and on the bomb run ten 'Oscars' from the 64th Sentai and five 'Nicks' from the 21st Sentai attacked the bombers in another running battle lasting 45 minutes. The bombers claimed four fighters destroyed and two probables, but the 492nd lost one of its new B-24Js when, having already lost an engine in the attack, the Liberator was struck by Cpl Tomio Kamiguchi's Ki-43-II near the waist gunners' position. The B-24 broke in half, and only the bombardier bailed out. Kamiguchi survived, however, having taken to his parachute. His exploits were widely reported by the Japanese press, who dubbed him 'Corporal Saw' because he had 'cut up the bomber with his propeller'.

November proved to be another tough month for the 7th BG as the Japanese continued to concentrate their efforts against the B-24s. The Tenth Air Force launched its heaviest raids to date against Rangoon,

B-24Ds from the 9th and 493rd BSs await their turn to take off from Pandaveswar on a mission in the autumn of 1943 (*3A-33640, RG342FH, NARA*)

as Maj Gen Stratemeyer wanted to destroy several of the most important installations around the city that had heretofore been merely damaged. He proposed to Air Chief Marshal Sir Richard Peirse that the Tenth and the RAF cooperate in a series of day and night bombing missions, to which Peirse agreed. To add strength to the Tenth Air Force, Stratemeyer asked Maj Gen Claire Chennault to lend him the 308th BG from the Fourteenth Air Force for these missions (see Chapter 4).

Targets were chosen with care, with the Insein locomotive works – the only facility in Burma capable of repairing locomotive engines – given priority. The second priority target was the Botataung docks on the Rangoon River. RAF Wellingtons and Liberators would bomb the Mahlwagon marshalling yards by night.

For the first time in the campaign, the B-24s would have fighter escorts all the way to the target. The 459th FS had arrived in-theatre with P-38 Lightnings, while the 311th Fighter Bomber Group lent its P-51A-equipped 530th FS. Stratemeyer planned to begin the missions on 25 November, with the offensive lasting one week.

In the run up to the Rangoon offensive the 7th BG undertook several large-scale attacks on the Japanese airfields at Mingaladon and Heho.

On the mission to the latter base on 11 November, seven Ki-43-IIs and two Ki-45s attacked the 9th BS's formation of six aircraft over the target. As one of the Hayabusas came in for a head-on pass at the aeroplane flown by Lt Ben Graves (a new B-24J that was in the No 3 position in the second element), flight engineer TSgt Doug Labat opened fire from the top turret. He poured out a long burst at the approaching fighter, but at the same moment a shell fired by the 'Oscar' struck the bomber's cockpit. Labat heard the sound of the explosive round going off and then felt a rush of cold air and flying debris around his legs.

He dropped out of his turret to find out what had happened. 'It was bad', he later recalled. 'Blood was splattered over everything, and maps and papers were flying around as air blasted through the shell hole in the windscreen. Co-pilot Lt Cy Kurth was slumped forward over the stick, while Graves was wavering in his seat. We were dropping fast'. The explosive shell had killed Kurth instantly and seriously wounded Graves. Labat dragged Kurth out of the co-pilot's seat, climbed in and brought the bomber out of its dive and back to level flight. Recovering consciousness, Graves told Labat to return to his turret, where Labat fought off a Ki-45 making a head-on pass.

The navigator, Lt Grant Erwin, came up to the cockpit to dress Graves' wounds. Erwin took over flying until the fighters had left, then changed places with Labat so that he could navigate the bomber back to base. On the downwind leg to land, the crew could not get the undercarriage down. Labat switched places with Lt Erwin and managed to get the emergency hand crank working that saw the landing gear extended. He then raced back to the cockpit to help Graves and Erwin land the aeroplane. As the big bomber rolled to a stop the pilot passed out. For their efforts in saving their aeroplane Graves, Labat and Erwin were all recommended for the Silver Star.

Three days later the 9th BS flew a joint mission with the 493rd to bomb the barracks in the town of Maymyo. With the primary target obscured by cloud, Maj Wesley Werner, the 493rd's commander, flew to the secondary target at Pakkoku. Here the bombers ran into at least seven Ki-43-IIs from the 50th Sentai, which began making frontal attacks. These went on for an hour, during which time three of the fighters were shot down – Sgt Sato, Sgt Maj Ofusa and Lt Hagashima all bailed out – while a fourth pilot was forced to crash land.

Three of the six 493rd BS aircraft were shot down. Lt George Kimball's aeroplane was hit and dove straight into the ground. With two engines out and his aeroplane smoking, Maj Werner headed west, closely followed by Lt Willis McLoughlin's heavily damaged Liberator. West of the Chindwin River, Werner's bomber crashed when its wing hit a tree as he was attempting a crash-landing, killing the entire crew. McLoughlin was somewhat luckier, as eight of his ten-man crew managed to survive the crash-landing of their aeroplane. Tragically, six of them would subsequently die in captivity as prisoners of the Japanese.

The series of missions to Rangoon began on 25 November as planned, but the day went badly. 9th BS aircraft were the first to take off from Pandaveswar at 0500 hrs and tragedy struck when two of the unit's B-24Js crashed moments after departure, killing the crews. The two squadrons from the 308th BG that were temporarily sharing the field with the 9th and 493rd BSs conducted their mission briefing with the depressing sound of explosions in the background.

Bombs from a 436th BS Liberator explode in the Botataung dock area of Rangoon during the mission on 28 November 1943 (*3A-37743, RG342FH, NARA*)

Bad weather around the Rangoon area covered the primary targets, which were the Insein locomotive workshops and the airfields at Mingaladon and Zayatkwin, so the two B-24 groups headed for their secondary target at Akyab instead, but not before flak had damaged an aircraft from the 493rd BS, which failed to make it back to base. Two P-51As from the 530th FS were also shot down in clashes with the 64th Sentai. By day's end three bombers had been lost with little to show for the effort. Worst of all, the element of surprise was gone.

The weather cleared sufficiently on 27 November for both bomb groups to target the Insein locomotive workshops once again. The combined formation sent aloft numbered 56 B-24s – the largest bombing mission to date in the CBI Theatre. Escorted by Lightnings and Mustangs, it made an impressive sight for the crews involved. The 3rd Chutai of the 64th Sentai rose to intercept the formation, committing eight Ki-43-IIs and one Ki-44. Four Ki-45s from the 21st Sentai also joined in. Despite being intercepted on the bomb run, the bombers achieved excellent results, with an estimated 70 per cent of the Insein facility destroyed or severely damaged.

In the air battle that followed the 308th BG had two B-24s shot down. In the 493rd BS's formation one aircraft had two engines knocked out, but it still managed to make a successful crash-landing off the Indian coast. The bombers and the fighter escort claimed 13 enemy fighters destroyed, with more probably destroyed or damaged, but the Japanese actually lost a Ki-43-II, the sole Ki-44 and a Ki-45.

The two groups returned to Rangoon the next day to target the Botataung dock area, making their bomb run from 19,000 ft and again doing considerable damage. Six Ki-43-IIs from the 64th Sentai and four Ki-45s from the 21st Sentai intercepted the formation, but they only succeeded in inflicting minor damage despite continuously attacking the B-24s for more than an hour. These poor results were testament to how difficult it was for the 'Oscar' to shoot down a Liberator. The bombers claimed several fighters destroyed and damaged, but none were lost. It was a long mission, with the bombers taking off at 0700 hrs and returning at 1800 hrs.

After two days for maintenance and repairs, the two bomb groups returned to Insein on 1 December, with 15 P-38s as escort. By an unfortunate coincidence, the JAAF's 5th Hikodan, which was preparing for a large raid on Calcutta, had ordered additional fighters to concentrate around Rangoon. More than 40 'Oscars' from the 64th and newly-arrived 204th Sentais and some ten Ki-45s from the 21st Sentai took off to intercept the American bombers. The 7th BG squadrons were on a north-to-south run to the target at 19,000 ft when they ran into heavy anti-aircraft fire and fighters. The latter attacked out of the sun approximately ten minutes before the bomb release point, using their standard frontal attack tactics. The fighters were in a firing position before they were spotted.

The 493rd BS was leading the 7th BG, with 21 aircraft in the first wave. Its B-24s were attacked first, and Lt Granville Stringfellow's aeroplane, in the lead position, was hit in the right wing by flak. As the pilot banked away from the formation, his bomber was quickly set upon by JAAF fighters. The Liberator was seen to fall apart in a ball of flames.

Liberators head for the Insein locomotive works on 1 December 1943. The 7th BG would lose five aircraft shot down that day (*7th BG(H) Historical Foundation, USAFA McDermott Library*)

The 9th BS took the brunt of the attack. Although its elements were flying the B-24J that day, the front turrets did not provide the hoped-for defensive fire. The lead bomber, flown by squadron operations officer Capt Bill Wright, was quickly shot down, followed by a second Liberator. The formation closed up, but a third aircraft was hit and fell away after repeated passes from the fighters. In the 436th BS formation, flak hit the wing of 2Lt John McLauchlen's bomber. When he dove off to the left, three 'Oscars' flown by Capt Yasuhiko Kuroe and WOs Tadashi Kinoshita and Yamazaki – attacked the bomber and shot it down.

This was the 7th BG's worst combat loss of the war (five aircraft shot down and five more seriously damaged), with the group having lost 12 bombers during November and December. Only ten of the 50 crewmen aboard the five aeroplanes shot down on 1 December managed to bail out. The 308th BG also lost a bomber that day. The Japanese fighters claimed ten B-24s shot down for the loss of two Ki-43-IIs and several more damaged.

The American contribution to the Rangoon offensive ended on 4 December with a successful mining mission to the Rangoon and Moulmein harbours. The RAF continued to fly night bombing missions for several more days. Apart from the locomotive works at Insein, which were severely damaged, the raids on Rangoon did not accomplish the level of destruction that had been hoped for, but they had brought a new level of cooperation between the Tenth Air Force and the RAF which was to be formalised two weeks later.

The crew of Lt Granville Stringfellow (standing on the right) from the 493rd BS. Flying a brand new B-24J, Stringfellow and his men were shot down and killed on the 1 December 1943 mission to Insein. Stringfellow's regular co-pilot, Lt Lynn Stokes, standing left, was not flying that day (*7th BG(H) Historical Foundation, USAFA McDermott Library*)

The groundcrew pose with their B-24J-15-CO 42-73158 *PECKER RED*. This aircraft, assigned to the 493rd BS, was one of the longest serving Liberators in the 7th BG. Indeed, it flew with the 493rd from the autumn of 1943 until May 1945 (*7th BG(H) Historical Foundation, USAFA McDermott Library*)

STRATEGIC AIR FORCE

At the Quadrant Conference held in Quebec in August 1943 and the Sextant Conference held three months later in Cairo, Roosevelt, Churchill and the combined chiefs of staff agreed on a more offensive strategy for Burma and to the setting up of a unified Allied command structure. Adm Lord Louis Mountbatten was appointed Supreme Commander of Southeast Asia Command (SEAC) and given the mission of capturing northern Burma to increase the flow of supplies to China.

The creation of SEAC finally brought about the integration of Tenth Air Force and RAF units in the India-Burma Theatre into Air Command, Southeast Asia under Air Marshal Sir Richard Peirse, with the operational units formed into the Eastern Air Command under Maj Gen Stratemeyer. Eastern Air Command was further divided into the Third Tactical Air Force and the Strategic Air Force, under Brig Gen Howard Davidson, which combined all USAAF and RAF heavy and medium bomber units together, joining the 7th BG with the Wellington and Liberator squadrons of No 231 Group, RAF. For the first time the operations of the strategic bomber force could be coordinated under one command making better use of the limited number of heavy bombers available. The Strategic Air Force was activated on 15 December 1943.

The mission of the Strategic Air Force was straightforward – to damage the Japanese transportation system so as to restrict the flow of supplies to the Japanese Army in Burma, thereby reducing its ability to resist the Allied armies' advances planned for 1944. The first priority remained Japanese shipping, with the second priority the rail communications network leading into Burma from Thailand and Malaya.

As the Strategic Air Force expanded its attacks on shipping and mining operations to ports in southern Burma and Thailand, the Japanese resorted to landing their ships at Singapore or Saigon and transporting supplies overland. As the flow of equipment shifted away from Rangoon, this increased the Japanese reliance on the rail network, and their vulnerability to its disruption. Railway stations and marshalling yards remained key targets for the Strategic Air Force, but as the year wore on the bombers devoted more and more of their effort to attacking the single track line from Thailand to Burma. The bombers began making low altitude attacks to create breaks in the railway line at numerous points.

What made these new tactics possible was the achievement of air superiority over most of Burma. RAF Spitfires had wrested control over the frontlines from the Japanese fighter force, which suffered heavy losses in air battles over the Arakan and around Imphal, while the counter-air operations of the Tenth Air Force's long-range P-38s and P-51s destroyed

B-24J *Lost Angel* was one of the first natural metal Liberators assigned to the 7th BG. This aeroplane brought its crew home from a mission on only two engines (*3A-34769, RG342FH, NARA*)

Japanese fighters and bombers both in the air and on the ground. During 1944 the 7th BG would lose just five aircraft to Japanese fighters.

STRATEGIC AIR FORCE MISSIONS

The Rangoon raids had shown that in the face of a strengthened Japanese fighter force the bombers would need fighter escort to continue daytime missions to targets in the area. It would be some time before the 7th BG returned to Rangoon. The spike in combat losses had an impact on morale, but two successful long range missions to Bangkok on the nights of 21 and 23 December went some way to restore it. All four squadrons went out on the 21st to bomb the dock areas and returned on the 23rd to hit the main railway station, bombing from 7800 ft to 9500 ft.

With the new year came new targets and new missions under the auspices of the Strategic Air Force, which had the 7th BG avoid daytime raids on targets where the bombers were likely to encounter strong fighter opposition. The B-24s flew to other targets and conducted more night missions to avoid the Japanese fighters. The group's squadrons had not received sufficient replacements to make up for their losses incurred during the last few months of 1943 and transfers of personnel at the end of their combat tours or to new assignments. As a result for the first few months of 1944 the units were short of combat crews – some had only seven crews available – and could rarely send out more than three to five aircraft on a mission. Group missions now consisted of 16 to 18 B-24s.

Japanese shipping remained the number one priority. The Japanese could no longer risk sending their larger freighters directly to Rangoon or even to Bangkok. Instead, the vessels would go to smaller ports along the southern Burma coast or to anchorages in the Gulf of Siam, where their cargos would be off-loaded to smaller ships or onto trains. In response, the Strategic Air Force conducted strikes on these smaller targets and expanded mining operations.

On 23 January all four squadrons flew 2400 miles to attack shipping at the port of Mergui, on the Burma coast. Capt Benjamin Joy,

Operations Officer of the 436th BS, had requested permission to bomb a large freighter reported to be in the harbour from low level. The unit missed the freighter on their bomb run but managed to strafe two smaller ships, sinking one and setting the other on fire. The remaining three squadrons, bombing from 8000 ft in the face of intense anti-aircraft fire, achieved several direct hits and near misses. Coming off the target, Joy's aeroplane was attacked by a single 'Oscar'. A fire broke out in the B-24, and the other crews saw Joy's bomber descend trailing smoke until it crashed on the shore a few miles away. There was only one survivor.

The next shipping strike came on the night of 7 March when three squadrons went out to attack vessels in ports in southern Burma and in the Gulf of Siam, each aeroplane carrying five 1000-lb bombs and a bomb-bay fuel tank to extend the range. These were long, tiring, 15-hour or more missions. In the target area the B-24s, which flew separately, would descend to 300 ft above the sea. The bombers left India in the late afternoon and returned to base the following morning.

The 436th BS sent three aircraft out that night, two to Mergui and one to the Gulf of Siam. Seeing no shipping, they ended up bombing the dock area at Tavoy. The 492nd and 493rd BSs sortied three and four aircraft respectively to sweep the area around Koh Si Chang – a small island southeast of Bangkok in the Gulf of Siam that the Japanese were using as an anchorage. Two aircraft from the 492nd bombed oil tanks and jetties on the island, as well as one ship. Running low on fuel, the third aircraft bombed the docks at Martaban, then on the return flight had to crash-land on a beach some 20 miles south of Calcutta. The 493rd had better luck, scoring direct hits on two freighters of 300 ft and 200 ft in length, both of which sank immediately.

A group mission to attack a Japanese convoy at Port Blair, in the Andaman Islands, on 15 April proved more costly. The four squadrons sent out 12 aircraft, which only managed to achieve several near misses on shipping in the harbour. The 'Oscars' of the 1st Chutai 26th Sentai, which were temporarily stationed on the island, intercepted the formation and in repeated passes managed to shoot down one aircraft from the 9th BS, which crashed into the sea.

Mining operations proved to be a more effective means of disrupting Japanese shipping. Mines would not only sink vessels, they could bring

A B-24J from the 436th BS comes in to land at Madhaiganj, in India, in early 1944 soon after the 7th BG had adopted colourful tail markings to identify its squadrons. The 436th applied yellow and black chequers to the fins of its Liberators (*3A-33739, RG342FH, NARA*)

shipping to a halt. Once a harbour had been mined, no shipping could enter or leave until the area had been swept clear of mines, which meant that supplies could not be off-loaded, vital shipping remained idle and sailing schedules were completely thrown off. Mining missions to the ports of southern Burma and over the Gulf of Siam were flown at night.

The squadrons would send out three to four aircraft, each taking off at five-minute intervals and then flying 1200 miles to mine a specific area. The harbours at Mergui and Tavoy, the Chao Phya River at Bangkok and the anchorages at Koh Si Chang and Sattahip, in the Gulf of Thailand, became regular stops on the schedule of mining missions. These sorties were not without incident. For example, an aircraft of the 436th BS arrived over Koh Si Chang only to find that the B-24's bomb release mechanism would not work. The bombardier, a Lt Eldridge, went back into the bomb-bay to release the mines manually in five separate runs over the designated area using a screwdriver.

On a mission to mine Sattahip harbour on 8 May 1944, the 9th BS's CO, Maj David Kellogg, had the misfortune to fly over a Japanese gunboat that he had not seen until it was too late to avoid. The alert enemy gunners sent a stream of 20 mm shells into the bomber as it passed overhead, setting the wing on fire and knocking out two engines. Kellogg had to ditch the aeroplane immediately, and only he and one of his gunners survived the crash.

With the second highest priority assigned to the communications network leading to and within Burma, the Japanese rail system received considerable attention. During January and February the 7th BG flew night missions to bomb the stations and marshalling yards at Bangkok, Moulmein and Mandalay, after which it began training for attacks on the Burma-Thailand railway. During February the squadrons took time off from their regular missions to conduct extensive training in low level attacks on railway lines, practising on the India lines around Bengal. The squadrons performed both formation and individual attacks.

The first low level mission against the Burma-Thailand railway took place on 23 March. Each squadron was assigned a section of line, but only the 9th and 436th BSs reached their target areas, attacking at dusk. The 492nd and 493rd BSs turned back due to bad weather and bombed their alternate targets. The 9th achieved the best results, destroying three bridges along the line and strafing six freight wagons.

The squadrons returned to the Burma-Thailand railway on 5 April, this time with more success. The bombers had to descend to 300 ft, manoeuvring below the nearby hills to hit their targets. The 9th and 436th BSs struck rail bridges while the 492nd and 493rd BSs were assigned the task of destroying sections of track. The 9th BS was

Maj David Kellogg, 9th BS CO, kneeling at right with his crew and their aeroplane, B-24J *Leaping Lena*. Kellogg would be shot down in this aircraft on 8 May 1944 (*7th BG(H) Historical Foundation, USAFA McDermott Library*)

again successful, destroying two bridges and strafing locomotives, rolling stock and buildings along their section of the line, but it lost one aircraft to flak. The bombardier, 2Lt Gene Gambale, and one gunner survived the crash. Gambale was later beaten to death whilst a PoW.

After successfully bombing several bridges, the three aeroplanes from the 436th BS strafed locomotives and buildings along their section of the line. The 493rd used 100-lb 'spike' bombs for the first time to blow up sections of track. The Tenth Air Force had found that standard bombs dropped on railway tracks at low altitude simply bounced off them. Through experimentation it was found that a three-foot long steel spike attached to the nose of the bomb would ensure that it penetrated the tracks. Three aircraft from the 493rd scored ten direct hits each along an eight-mile section of the track. The flight leader, Capt Bailey, had an engine shot out, a second damaged and a gunner killed by flak on his bomb run. He was forced to ditch his B-24 in the Bay of Bengal on the return flight, all the remaining crew being rescued the next day by a PBY.

In the final mission against the rail network before the monsoons began, the 7th BG, in cooperation with the RAF, sent out 12 aircraft to block the southern entrance of the Mandalay marshalling yards. The bombing on this occasion was excellent, trapping both locomotives and rolling stock in the yards so that RAF Beaufighters could strafe them.

The Strategic Air Force's third priority for attack was the JAAF's airfields in Burma, the 'heavies' making a contribution to the counter-air operations of the Tenth's long-range fighters. During February and March the 7th BG conducted several night missions against the airfields at Aungban, Heho, Mingaladon, Hmawbi and Zayatkwin around Rangoon, as well as daytime missions to the airfields at Loiwing and Akyab. The nocturnal missions were small raids, each squadron sending out only three to five aeroplanes a night, taking off at five-minute intervals and bombing individually from medium altitudes.

For the most part, during these missions the bombers faced searchlights and anti-aircraft fire that was usually described as meagre, but the airfields around Rangoon were more heavily defended. The Japanese had no nightfighters available in Burma, but the 'Oscars' of the 204th Sentai had managed several successful interceptions at night working in cooperation with searchlights in and around Rangoon and Mingaladon, claiming two RAF Liberators on the night of 29 February 1944.

On the night of 4 March, the 493rd BS sent off four aircraft to bomb Zayatkwin airfield. Only one found the target, but a second Liberator made a bomb run on Mingaladon from 15,900 ft. Coming in over the field, 15 searchlights coned the bomber and held it for eight minutes. Up to six 'Oscars' attacked the bomber from below, making eight passes from the front, side and rear quarters. Despite taking evasive action in the form of diving and climbing turns, and then a violent corkscrew, the aeroplane was held by searchlights until it was out of range. Remarkably, the B-24 received only minor damage from these attacks.

Japanese Army supply dumps and military installations were a lower priority for the Strategic Air Force, but the 7th BG found itself increasingly called on to support Allied ground forces as a result of both Japanese and Allied offensives. To forestall expected 14th Army advances into Burma, the Japanese launched their own offensives in the Arakan in February (Operation *Ha-Go*) and against Imphal in mid-March, (Operation *I-Go*).

The Allies had begun their own offensive actions, with the second Chindit expedition, Operation *Thursday*, beginning on 5 March in support of Lt Gen Stilwell's Chinese and American force moving down the Hukwang and Mogaung valleys in northeastern Burma toward the vital town of Myitkyina. The first of the 7th BG's ground support missions was on 17 January 1944. After two previous attempts had failed due to weather, the 9th, 492nd and 493rd BSs bombed Japanese barracks and troop concentrations at Kyaukchaw, some 90 miles southeast of Imphal. Bombing from 10,500 ft the formation blanketed the target area, the 493rd dropping 60 325-lb depth charges.

During March the group flew eight missions in support of the 14th Army, bombing supply dumps across a wide area of Burma. One of these missions saw dumps around Victoria Lake, in Rangoon, targeted at night. For this mission two aircraft from the 436th BS acted as pathfinders, lighting up the target area for the following squadrons, who ran into searchlights, heavy anti-aircraft fire and three to four 'Oscars' attempting to make interceptions. The mission was a success, with returning crews reporting fires visible 35 miles away from the target.

On 26 March the 14th Army asked the 7th BG to bomb a section of the Tiddim-Imphal Road where the 17th Division was engaged in a fighting withdrawal back to Imphal. The group sent out nine aircraft, but only the element from the 436th BS managed to clearly identify the target area and bomb it successfully.

Ground support missions continued up to the end of May, when the monsoon weather began to interfere with operations. One of the last missions, on 10 May, was a night attack on Myitkyina to cover the approach of Stilwell's forces. The 436th BS recorded that its three aircraft dropped 12 500-lb bombs, 48 100-lb bombs and 200 beer bottles!

During the first two weeks of June the squadrons attempted a number of missions into Burma, but most were turned back due to adverse weather. Replacement combat crews had finally begun to arrive in May, with more due in June, so that all four squadrons were either back up to full strength, or close to it, by mid 1944.

On 13 June the 7th BG received a bombshell. Maj Gen Stratemeyer and Brig Gen Davidson visited all four squadrons to inform them that effective immediately the group would be relieved from bombing operations during the monsoon season and converted to transporting fuel to the Fourteenth Air Force, which was desperately trying to stem the *Ichi-Go* offensive in China (see Chapter Five). The 7th would lose more B-24s flying the 'Hump' route than it would lose in combat that year.

The shift from bombing to 'hauling gas' was something of a let down for most crews, especially for the bombardiers who were all grounded. To save weight the ball turrets on the B-24Js were removed and the crew size cut from ten to seven – pilot, co-pilot, navigator, flight engineer, radio operator and two gunners. Each Liberator was fitted with three 420-gallon bomb-bay tanks. The specified maximum gross weight for the B-24J was 65,000 lbs. The 7th BG's squadrons had been routinely flying at 68,000 lbs, and they would soon be managing take-offs at 70,000 lbs.

The Hollywood movie actress Paulette Goddard prepares to christen a new 492nd BS B-24J in April 1944. This aeroplane was lost on a 'gas hauling' mission over the 'Hump' four months later (*7th BG(H) Historical Foundation, USAFA McDermott Library*)

In a memoir he wrote after the war, Bradley Hamlett, who flew 'gas hauling' missions from China at the end of the year with the 436th BS, recalled that the take-off procedure involved setting the manifold pressure well above the recommended level and, as speed built up down the runway, raising the nose just enough to get the nose wheel off the ground. When the aeroplane reached the end of the runway, 'you would gently ease back on the control column and hope the SOB would fly'.

The change in role began immediately. The group's squadrons were assigned to bases to the east of Calcutta, trading places with a B-25 unit. The 9th and 493rd BSs went to Kurmitola while the 436th and 492nd BSs were sent to Tezagon. For the next week the four squadrons ran a daily shuttle transporting men and equipment to their new bases. 'Gas hauling' missions began on 20 June 1944 and continued until the end of September, with three to seven aeroplanes going out nearly every day.

The flights were hard work. Pilots were often on instruments for six or more hours, flying through heavy rain, icing and turbulence. Aeroplanes were lost with depressing regularity to a variety of causes – weather, mechanical problems and crashes on take-off when heavily overloaded. Two aeroplanes were lost in June, five in July, five in August and two in September. In most cases, but not always, the crews managed to bail out and were rescued. For some reason the 492nd suffered the most, losing six B-24s. The last 'gas hauling' mission was flown on 30 September, and with relief the squadrons returned to their true mission of bombing the Japanese, having carried more than 2,000,000 gallons of fuel over the 'Hump' to China.

It took another week of shuttle runs to bring the 9th and 493rd BSs back to their base at Pandaveswar and the 436th and 492nd BSs to nearby Madhaiganj. All four units spent the next ten days in an intensive refresher training programme for all combat crews. New aeroplanes began to arrive in the form of M- and L-model Liberators.

Not having flown in formation for several months, pilots and co-pilots practised such flying in three-aeroplane elements and six-aeroplane squadron flights, while bombardiers and gunners brushed up their special skills with practice bomb runs and aerial firing. To give their gunners a more realistic target, the 492nd sent pairs of B-24s out over the Bay of Bengal. One aircraft would fly a steady course at 1500 ft while the second machine made runs from different directions with its gunners firing at the first bomber's shadow on the water.

The 7th BG spent June through to September 1944 'hauling gas' to China. B-24J-185-CO 44-40852 from the 436th BS is seen here on the ramp at Kunming after completing one such flight. The third Liberator in the line up is a veteran B-24D. A handful of these aircraft soldiered on into the autumn of 1944 (*3A-00980, RG342FH, NARA*)

As the scoreboard on *"Old 86"/THE LIMITED EXPRESS* illustrates, the 7th BG interrupted its bombing missions to fly gasoline over the 'Hump' during the 1944 monsoon season. This aircraft would ultimately fly more than 1300 hrs with the 492nd BS (*SQ-Bomb-492-HI-May 1945, AFHRA*)

B-24J-155-CO *SHOOT YOU'RE COVERED* was a late model Liberator that flew with the 9th BS (*7th BG(H) Historical Foundation, USAFA McDermott Library*)

The first mission after resuming bombing operations was a group attack on docks and railway jetties at Moulmein on 19 October. The 7th BG was joined by RAF Liberator VIs from No 356 Sqn for the first joint daylight raid conducted by the Allies. The group sent out 24 aircraft from all four squadrons and their bombing was reasonably good.

However, the target had not been totally destroyed, so a second mission was scheduled for 22 October, again involving 24 aircraft from the 9th, 492nd and 493rd BSs and No 356 Sqn Liberator VIs. The bombers went in at noon at 7800 ft and bombed with excellent results, scoring many direct hits in the target area. Just after completing the bomb run, 12 Ki-43-IIs from the 64th Sentai hit the 493rd BS formation, and they continued to attack for the next 30 minutes. The 'Oscars' made repeated individual passes mostly from the front quarter, pressing home their attacks. Lt Donald Blair's aeroplane was hit in the No 2 engine, which was set on fire. He pulled out of the formation and managed to get the engine fire out, but was last seen going into clouds with a fighter attacking his damaged aircraft. Although no trace of Blair's bomber or crew were ever found, the 64th Sentai pilots reported shooting the aeroplane down into a swamp near Bassein.

Next to be hit was the B-24 of Maj Jack Bradford, who was flying in the slot position of a four-aeroplane element. Hit in a head-on attack, Bradford swung his bomber out of formation down and to the left, but then tried to get back into position. As he brought his aeroplane back up he ran into the No 3 B-24 flown by 1Lt Arthur Bodmer. The tail of Bradford's aeroplane sliced into the bomb-bay area of Bodmer's Liberator and seconds later Bodmer's propellers chewed the tail off Bradford's aircraft. Both B-24s crashed into the sea with no survivors.

For the next several months the 7th BG would alternate missions such as this against Japanese supply dumps, airfields, railway yards and other targets over Burma and Thailand with what became the group's specialty in the final months of the war in Burma – busting bridges. In the four months from January to April 1945, with full complements of crews and aeroplanes, the 7th BG would drop more bombs than it had during all of 1943.

With the 14th Army's advance into Burma following the crushing defeat of the Japanese at Imphal, and a strong likelihood that this

advance would continue all the way to Rangoon in 1945, the Strategic Air Force concentrated on breaking enemy lines of communication in southern Burma, Thailand and Malaya. Bridges became a vital target in this campaign, for every time one was destroyed or damaged along the extensive single track railway lines into Burma, traffic ground to a halt. The more bridges that could be knocked down, and for longer periods, the greater the disruption to the flow of supplies to the retreating Japanese armies.

Bridges were never easy targets. An analysis of the bombing effort during 1943 had shown that the Liberators had managed to achieve only one direct hit on a bridge for every 81 sorties, and these were targets that required direct hits – near misses did little damage to a bridge's structure. The 7th BG would resort to medium and low level attacks, new tactics and a new weapon in its offensive against bridges in Thailand and Burma.

Towards the end of 1944 the 7th BG began a sustained campaign against the Japanese rail network that connected Burma with Thailand. This offensive would continue until the liberation of Burma in May 1945. Here, a second bypass bridge to the right of the main bridge and the first bypass comes under attack (3A-37567, RG342FH, NARA)

The first operation against bridges was a volunteer mission on 1 November 1944 to bomb the Ban Dara Bridge in central Thailand on the line from Bangkok to Chiang Mai. The Japanese Army had been steadily building up the flow of supplies along this northern route as an alternative to the main line west from Bangkok to Burma. Four aircraft,

CABIN IN THE SKY, a late model B-24J from the 492nd BS, undergoes maintenance at Madhaiganj in early 1945 (*SQ-Bomb-492-HI-March 1945, AFHRA*)

one from each squadron, attacked the bridge an hour before sunset, each Liberator making individual runs at 300 ft and dropping one 1000-lb bomb on each run. After three aeroplanes had finished their bomb runs, the bridge was still standing. Lt Nemecek of the 436th BS came in to make his last run and hit one of the bridge's main concrete piers with three 1000-lb bombs, dropping the 800 ft bridge into the river below.

While the 9th and 493rd BSs withdrew from operations for two weeks to undergo intensive training in low level attacks, the 436th and 492nd BSs kept up the campaign

against the bridges, running several missions against structures on the Bangkok-Chiang Mai line, with mixed success. The crews, bombing from different altitudes, would often see their bridge target completely covered with explosions, only to find that it was still standing when the dust and smoke cleared. Knowing that the bombers would have to come back, the Japanese moved machine guns in to defend the Kaeng Luang Bridge and on the repeat attack on 21 November shot down Lt Mead's aircraft as he ran in on the target at 300 ft, killing the entire crew.

At the end of November the 9th and 493rd BSs sent 12 and nine aircraft respectively to bomb Bridge 277 on the Bangkok-Moulmein railway line. This structure spanned the infamous River Kwai, and despite achieving a tight bomb pattern from 8500 ft, the bridge was left standing. The 9th BS tried again on 13 December in cooperation with the 436th BS. While the latter unit bombed the flak batteries nearby, the 9th sent in 12 aircraft from medium altitude and two at low level.

The B-24s also went in to bomb bridges at low level. Here, the Bilin rail bridge on the Burma-Thailand railway is under attack (*3A-37527, RG342FH, NARA*)

Having knocked the Bilin rail bridge into the river below, this 436th BS B-24 heads off in search of another target in early 1945 (*3A-37525, RG342FH, NARA*)

The execution was flawless, but once again the bridge remained standing. It would be attacked so often that the structure would become known within the 7th BG as 'Old 277'. After returning from his fourth or fifth mission to 'Old 277', one crewman 'volunteered to parachute out and dynamite the damn thing'.

'Old 277' finally fell on 13 February, when four B-24s from the 493rd BS, followed by six aeroplanes from the 9th BS, finally managed to bring the bridge down with a low level attack at 300 ft.

Part of the solution to the problem of bombing bridges came with the introduction of a new weapon, the Azon bomb. This was a 1000-lb bomb with a radio-controlled tail fin that allowed the bombardier to manoeuvre the weapon after it had been dropped to correct deflection errors in flight. A flare attached to the rear of the bomb enabled the bombardier to track its fall. Azon bombs were ideal for attacking the narrow bridges on the Burma-Thailand railway line in the clear weather of the dry season.

Bridges proved difficult to destroy with regular bombs, so in December 1944 the 7th BG began using radio-controlled Azon bombs which proved far more effective. A flare attached to the rear of the weapon, as shown in this photograph, allowed the bombardier to track the bomb's fall and steer it to the target (3A-37737, RG342FH, NARA)

B-24s equipped for Azon bombing were assigned to the 493rd BS. They could be identified by the three radio antennae on the underside of the rear fuselage below the tail section (SQ-Bomb-493-HI-March 1945, AFHRA)

In the autumn of 1944 ten B-24s equipped for Azon bombing and ten trained crews joined the 7th BG. Initially distributed among the four units, they were subsequently reassigned to the 493rd BS for ease of maintenance.

The first Azon mission took place on 27 December 1944, when six aircraft attacked the Pyinmana railway bridge in Burma. Four Azon bombs dropped the middle span and knocked the southern span to a 45-degree angle, while eight 2000-lb bombs landing within 100 ft of the bridge did little damage.

On its second Azon mission on 30 December the 493rd BS demonstrated how effective this new bomb could be. The group sent out all four squadrons to bomb the Taungup-Prome highway, the 493rd carrying Azon bombs and the other squadrons 2000-lb bombs. After demolishing one 325-ft long wooden trestle bridge with a combination of Azon and 2000-lb bombs, the 493rd blew up a 75-ft long bypass bridge nearby, and then followed the 9th BS to another 150-ft long bridge. The 9th failed to knock down the latter, so the 493rd came in and dropped it with Azon bombs in two runs. The unit then went to a 385-ft long bridge near Taungup, and with only four Azon bombs left, knocked the bridge out with three direct hits. From then on the 493rd BS concentrated on using the Azon bomb while the other units continued their attacks from medium and low level.

As January turned to February and February to March the list of destroyed and damaged bridges grew longer. On 19 March the 7th BG flew a bridge-busting mission that earned the group its second Distinguished Unit Citation. Some 37 B-24s from all four squadrons flew to the Kra Isthmus on the Malaya peninsula, several hundred miles

A 7th BG formation heads for Ramree Island, in the Bay of Begal, in February 1945. The Allies fought a pitched battle with the Japanese Army for occupation of the strategically important island in January-February 1945 (3A-33601, RG342FH, NARA)

south of Bangkok, to bomb bridges on the Bangkok-Singapore railway line. The bombers carried two bomb-bay fuel tanks and four 1000-lb bombs each. The mission involved a 19-hour round trip flight of 2700 miles, the 9th BS historian noting proudly that this was just 300 miles short of the longest B-29 mission to date. The group knocked out several key bridges and bombed rail facilities. One crewman was killed and two wounded by flak and an aeroplane ditched on the return flight when it ran out of fuel.

In April Col Harvey Alness, the 7th BG's commander, decided to

SHACKRAT Special **was a B-24J that flew with the 9th BS. In March 1945 the bomber completed its 50th mission without an abort (*7th BG(H) Historical Foundation, USAFA McDermott Library*)**

introduce a new bombing technique using a glide-bombing approach. A similar tactic had proved extremely successful for the B-25s of the 341st BG. The latter had discovered through a fortuitous accident that a form of glide-bombing with a sharp pull-up at the end of the glide could send a bomb directly into a bridge's structure instead of it bouncing off as had happened in many low level attacks. Thinking through the problem, Col Alness came up with the same solution.

Although the idea of using the Liberator as a dive-bomber seemed slightly insane to some, Col Alness had the 9th, 436th, and 492nd BSs go through a short but intensive training programme in the new technique, using a mock-up of a 200-ft long bridge. The pilot would approach the target along its long axis and then begin his glide at 1500 ft, descending in a 20- to 25-degree glide to release the bomb at 500 ft as he pulled out. A toggle switch was fitted to the control column so that the pilot could release the bomb using a special sight designed specifically for this purpose.

The 7th BG tried out the new bombing technique on 24 April 1945. The mission that day was to destroy as many bridges as possible along the Burma-Thailand railway, with each squadron given a designated section of the line. The group sent out 41 aeroplanes, the 493rd with its Azon bombs and the other three squadrons using glide-bombing. Up to this point the 7th BG had destroyed 98 bridges with its combination of medium and low altitude attacks and the newer Azon bombs.

The results on the 24 April mission were nothing short of spectacular for at least 30 bridges were destroyed and another 18 damaged, as well as large sections of railway track left buckled. Virtually every pilot sent out managed to destroy or damage a bridge.

The cumulative effect of the Strategic Air Force's bombing campaign against the bridges put a severe strain on the enemy in Burma. Allied intelligence had estimated that the Japanese Army needed approximately 490 tons of supplies a day, with JAAF units requiring an additional 110 tons. By the early months of 1945 the combined efforts of the 7th BG and RAF Liberator units in the Strategic Air Force had reduced the daily tonnage over the railway lines into Burma to less than 150 tons a day.

During the first week of May the group flew several missions in support of the capture of Rangoon and then turned to bombing the southern Burma ports of Martaban, Mergui and Tavoy to harry the retreating Japanese Army. The capture of Rangoon effectively brought an end to the campaign to liberate Burma. By prior agreement the Eastern Air

The 7th BG flew missions in support of the British 14th Army as it advanced toward Rangoon in early 1945. This B-24 from the 9th BS was photographed on its bomb run. The black rudder chequers synonymous with aircraft from this unit have yet to be applied to the Liberator (*7th BG(H) Historical Foundation, USAFA McDermott Library*)

Opposite top
B-24J-105-CF *Spirit of Fort Worth* was the last of 3034 J-model Liberators built at the Consolidated Fort Worth plant, coming off the line on 30 December 1944. Delivered to the 493rd BS, it was converted into an Azon bomber. The B-24 crashed on take-off at Dudkundi, India, in May 1945, but it was repaired, only to crash again at Abadan, Iran, during its return flight home in October 1945 (*3A-33638, RG342FH, NARA*)

Opposite bottom
All B-24s assigned to 'hauling gas' had the top and ball turrets and all other armament removed and three large bomb-bay fuel tanks installed (*SQ-Bomb-492-HI-June 1945, AFHRA*)

JUNGLE JIG **joined the 492nd BS in the autumn of 1943, and it was still flying in early 1945, having completed an impressive number of bombing and 'Hump' missions (***SQ-Bomb-492-HI-February 1945, AFHRA***)**

Command, and with it the Strategic Air Force, was dissolved and the units of the Tenth Air Force withdrawn from Burma in preparation for their move to China. For the 7th BG this brought a return, with the exception of the 493rd BS, to 'hauling gas' to China. As the 9th BS history recorded 'no single order ever as effectively depleted, in one stroke, the morale of

a unit'. Resigned to their fate in early June, the men of the 9th, 436th, and 492nd BSs moved to Tezpur, in northern Assam.

With the risk of Japanese fighters effectively eliminated, the B-24s were refitted to carry the maximum amount of fuel possible. The top and bottom turrets were removed and the nose and tail turrets stripped of armament. Flight crews were again cut back, to five, the bombardiers and all gunners being unnecessary for these flights, thus saving more weight (and more lives).

The squadrons were then sent to Jorhat to fly two missions over the 'Hump' with Air Transport Command (ATC) pilots. The pilots of the 492nd BS, who noted that 'we of the 7th BG use the word "hump" as an ordinary noun without undue capital letters', were not particularly impressed. The ATC pilots, they noted, 'take-off with a gross weight of 60,000 lbs. They don't know what it is like to take-off with a gross weight of 70,000 lbs or over'.

The three squadrons then began regular missions flying fuel into China for the Fourteenth Air Force. These missions lasted until the middle of September, the squadrons flying 120 to 140 flights a month with the loss of five aeroplanes and four crews. One aircraft from the 492nd BS

By the spring of 1945, the Allied air forces had established almost complete air superiority over Burma. As if to prove this point, a B-24 from the 492nd BS boldly flies past a Japanese airfield with no fear of interception (*7th BG(H) Historical Foundation, USAFA McDermott Library*)

Following the liberation of Burma in May 1945, the Strategic Air Force was disbanded. The 7th BG reassigned three of its squadrons to 'haul gas' over the 'Hump'. One of those units was the 492nd BS, which took up residence at Tezpur, in India, in June 1945 (*SQ-Bomb-492-HI-June 1945, AFHRA*)

Exempt from 'hauling gas', the 493rd BS continued to fly missions deep into Thailand by day and by night dropping propaganda leaflets. The squadron adorned many of its Liberators with a special high gloss black paint specifically for these missions (*SQ-Bomb-493-HI-August 1945, AFHRA*)

Lt A L Shindeldecker, kneeling second from right, and his crew with their Liberator, *THAI TIMES*, after a leaflet dropping mission over Thailand in August 1945 (*SQ-Bomb-493-HI-August 1945, AFHRA*)

(B-24J-200-CO 44-41223) set a squadron record by flying 48 missions over the 'Hump' during this period. Then came the welcome return to the United States.

The 493rd BS, meanwhile, had remained at Pandaveswar flying combat missions. From June to August the unit flew over much of Thailand dropping propaganda leaflets on major cities and towns. On the first mission into Thailand on 18 June, to drop medical supplies into Bangkok at the request of the pro-American Thai underground, the three aircraft sent out had an escort of 12 P-38s. However, with the complete absence of any aerial opposition, the escorts were dispensed with and the B-24s flew out on their own by day and by night, encountering only the occasional burst of anti-aircraft fire.

Initially these leaflet-dropping missions were combined with diversionary bombing raids on Japanese airfields in Thailand, but the raids were soon dropped. Usually, an element of three aircraft would take off at dawn to fly deep into Thailand to drop leaflets from low altitude, even flying directly over Bangkok in broad daylight. The 493rd's final mission was on 3 September when four aircraft dropped leaflets on 17 Thai towns.

In nearly three years of combat the B-24s of the 7th BG had dropped 13,165 tons of bombs in the course of nearly 500 combat missions and carried close to 3,000,000 gallons of fuel to China. The group lost 71 aeroplanes, 48 on combat missions and 23 on 'gas hauling' missions. In supporting the campaign to liberate Burma the USAAF units in the CBI Theatre had contributed to a major victory against the Japanese, and none more so than the 7th BG. The group had been in at the beginning and remained in action to the end. Time and again the B-24 had proven its worth with its range, its load capacity and its versatility.

FOURTEENTH AIR FORCE

America's primary objective in the CBI Theatre, and the rationale for its creation, was to increase the effectiveness of support to China for the prosecution of the war against Japan. As US military planners grappled with how best to achieve this objective given all the political, geographic and logistical complexities in the CBI, a debate emerged on the proper strategy to pursue. Lt Gen Stilwell adhered to the belief that re-opening a land route through China, with Chinese armies trained in India that could later be deployed in China for an offensive against the Japanese, was an absolute necessity and the only practical alternative. Stilwell doubted that the air route over the 'Hump' could replace land transportation.

Brig Gen Claire Chennault, commander of the CATF, was adamantly opposed to Stilwell's plan, arguing that the land route would take too long to complete and end up prolonging the war. Chennault proposed as an alternative a greatly strengthened American air force in China. He promised that with 500 aircraft he could destroy Japanese air power in China, thus setting the stage for the expected American landing on the China coast. More immediately, with more aircraft Chennault believed he could seriously disrupt the flow of Japanese shipping to and from the rest of Asia that went along the China coast. Anti-shipping strikes could prevent supplies from reaching the Japanese armies in the field and vital raw materials from reaching Japan's war industries.

At the Casablanca Conference in January 1943, Generalissimo Chiang Kai-Shek argued for the creation of an independent American air force in China that was led by Chennault as the first step toward implementing his air plan. Following the conference Gen Hap Arnold toured the CBI and visited China. He promised more support for Chennault, including the transfer of a heavy bomber group. On his return to Washington, DC, Arnold recommended that Chennault be given his own air force and on 10 March 1943 the Fourteenth Air Force was activated.

The benefit of Chennault's plan, as seen in early 1943, was its immediacy. An air campaign could begin relatively quickly, while Stilwell's proposals could not be put into effect until the end of 1943 at the earliest. Increasing American air power in China would be a welcome gesture of support to Chiang and the Chinese people, and it would give recognition to an American commander who had already conducted a brilliant air battle against the Japanese with the bare minimum of resources. With Chiang's strong advocacy Chennault won President Roosevelt's support for his air plan. In May Roosevelt agreed to provide more aircraft to Chennault's forces, and to devote the major proportion of 'Hump' tonnage to the new Fourteenth Air Force.

Chennault's air plan rested on two critical assumptions – first, that the flow of supplies over the 'Hump' route could be dramatically increased, and second, that his air bases in central and eastern China could be protected from any Japanese offensive. The US air units in China were totally dependent on air supply for every drop of gasoline, every bomb, every bullet and every spare part needed for their aeroplanes. For the entire war logistics dominated and dictated the Fourteenth Air Force's offensive capacity. Indeed, it could expand its offensive operations only to the extent that adequate amounts of supplies came over the 'Hump'.

Defence of the American air bases was another question. Stilwell believed that if the air campaign Chennault was proposing achieved the success he hoped for, the Japanese were likely to react violently and launch an offensive to capture Chennault's air bases. Better to have a trained and well-equipped army to defend these bases, Stilwell argued, before launching a major air campaign. Chennault accepted the possibility that the Japanese could launch an offensive, but doubted it would be successful. He placed full confidence in Generalissimo Chiang Kai-Shek's promise to defend the airfields. Logistics and defence of the airfields would have a profound impact on the operations of the 308th BG, which Arnold had promised to send to China.

308th BG BEGINS OPERATIONS

Chennault had three primary objectives for his new air force – the JAAF in China, Japanese Army and Navy installations in China and Japanese shipping and port facilities. As in Burma, there were few strategic targets in-theatre. Although long-range bombers would increase his striking power, Chennault was initially reluctant to accept a heavy bomber group for the Fourteenth Air Force because he feared the greater demands of the heavy bombers for fuel and ammunition would place undue strain on the 'Hump' supply route.

In early 1943 the flow of supplies over the 'Hump' was well below the amounts Chennault needed to expand his air offensive. The solution to this problem was to have the heavy bombers be self-supporting, flying their own supply missions that transported the gas and ammunition that they needed from India to China. So from the very beginning of its service in China, the 308th BG, unlike almost all other bomb groups in the USAAF, had a dual mission – hauling supplies over the 'Hump' and conducting combat operations.

The 308th BG was one of the many wartime groups hurriedly brought to life in the USAAC's rapid expansion after the attack on Pearl Harbor. The group was activated on 15 April 1942 with four component squadrons, the 373rd, 374th, 375th, and the 425th BSs. In September Col Eugene Beebe, who had previously served

A 308th BG B-24D takes off past a line-up of P-40Ks from the 23rd FG at Kunming in the spring of 1943. The gasoline from one Liberator could fill the tanks of more than 20 Warhawks (*RG208-AA-Box 108: Airplanes-Army-B-24-Exploits-China, NARA*)

as Hap Arnold's personal pilot, took command of the group, which was assigned B-24D Liberators. The 308th BG completed its phase training at the end of 1942, and early in the New Year it was alerted for overseas movement, receiving its full complement of new B-24Ds.

In early February Beebe learned that the group would be going to China, and on the 15th of that month it began the long flight from the United States down to Brazil, across the Atlantic and Africa to Karachi and then to the Tenth Air Force air depot at Agra, in India,

B-24D-20-CO 41-24166 *MISS CARRIAGE* was among the first group of Liberators to arrive in China, serving with the 373rd BS (*Peter M Bowers Collection, Museum of Flight*)

where all the bombers were thoroughly overhauled. Here, Cpl A C Mitchell added nose art to the B-24s at the request of many of the crews. Among the aeroplanes that emerged with new, personalised identities were *Axis Nightmare, Ubangi Bag, Dippy Dave and His 8 Dippy Diddlers, Snowball From Hell, MISS CARRIAGE, Hell's Angels, The Bad Penny, The Wolf* and the famous *The GOON*.

After a few weeks in India the entire air echelon of the 308th flew to China on 20 March, with the group HQ and the 425th BS going to Kunming, the 373rd BS to Yangkai, some 40 miles northeast of Kunming, and the 374th and 375th BSs to Chengkung, 12 miles southeast of Kunming. In a grim introduction to the challenges ahead, the aeroplane of Maj Robert Fensler, CO of the 425th BS, disappeared on the flight from India to China.

After settling in at their new bases, the 308th spent the month of April ferrying supplies to China from India, carrying everything the group would need to fly combat. Three B-24s were lost on these missions, which initially followed the direct ferry route between India and China,

The 308th BG flew its first combat mission on 4 May 1943 when it attacked targets in Samah Bay, on the south coast of Hainan Island (*Courtesy John V Osborne via the National Museum of the US Air Force*)

flying at 20,000-25,000 ft often through bad weather and severe icing. On 8 April, one of the group's aeroplanes was seen to crash ten miles from the field at Chabua, in Assam, spinning down out of the overcast without its tail. All on board perished. With more experience, the crews judged these missions to be 'more trying, about as dangerous and much less interesting than combat flights'.

It would take roughly three flights over the 'Hump' to accumulate enough supplies for one aircraft to fly a combat mission. By the beginning of May, the group had flown around 100,000 gallons

The 308th's second mission was on 8 May 1943 when it targeted the Tien-Ho airfield at Canton, leaving the barracks and storage areas burning (*3A-02626, RG342FH, NARA*)

of fuel and 200,000 lbs of 1000-lb and 500-lb bombs to China. With this stock in hand, the 308th was ready for combat.

On 4 May 1943, the group flew its first combat mission – a combined effort with the B-25s of the 11th BS that was protected by 15 P-40s. Eighteen B-24s, six each from the 373rd and 374th BSs and three apiece from the 375th and 425th BSs, accompanied the B-25s and the P-40s to Hanoi, in French Indochina, then flew farther on to bomb Japanese installations at Samah Bay, on the south coast of Hainan Island. The mission was a complete success, the bombers hitting docks and warehouses, the airfield and barracks. One aircraft from the 373rd BS ran out of fuel on the return flight, but the crew bailed out successfully 150 miles from Kunming and returned a few days later.

Four days later the group went out again with the B-25s to attack the Tien-Ho airfield at Canton. The 16 B-24s targeted the barracks and storage areas around the base while the B-25s hit the airfield, bombing from 18,000 ft to 24,000 ft. On its second run over the target, one flight of three aeroplanes from the 374th BS ran into 15 enemy fighters – most likely Ki-43-IIs from the 33rd Sentai, claiming three shot down. Following these two successful missions, the group returned to ferrying supplies over the 'Hump'. This operational pattern would continue until the spring of 1944 when the ATC became capable of taking over most of the supply flights.

At the end of May the 308th BG sent a contingent of six B-24s from the 374th BS and three from the 425th BS to Chengtu, northwest of Chunking, at the request of the Chinese Army to help counter a Japanese offensive that appeared to be aimed at Chunking. On 29 May, the nine bombers targeted the city of Ichang, and the day they hit Japanese artillery positions south of the city. On the 31st the nine aircraft, with a P-40 escort, set out to bomb the Japanese airfield at Kingmen, but cloud covered the target. After circling the area for 20 minutes, 20 JAAF fighters came up to intercept the formation but ran into the P-40 escort. The bombers then headed to the secondary target at Ichang, where they ran into another group of 'Oscar' fighters. In a running battle the B-24s from the 374th BS claimed ten fighters destroyed and the 425th BS another ten – a new record for bombers in China – although it appears highly likely that there was a certain amount of over-claiming.

B-24D-53-CO 42-40367 *China Doll* was photographed at the 425th BS base at Kunming. This aircraft was withdrawn from service on 4 February 1944 after being badly damaged in an accident (*RG208-AA-Box 108: Airplanes-Army-B-24-Exploits-China, NARA*)

In June the monsoon arrived, with torrential rains and cloud flooding airfields and covering targets. Apart from one aborted mission to Haiphong, where most aircraft were forced to bomb targets of opportunity due to the weather, during the month the 308th returned to ferrying supplies over the 'Hump'. Indeed, the group's aeroplanes flew 146 round trips to India in June. By mid-July the weather had improved sufficiently to resume flying combat missions. Chennault instructed the 308th BG to put priority on attacking enemy shipping and port facilities.

On 8 July the group sent out 22 aeroplanes to bomb the docks and nearby freighters in the French Indochinese port of Haiphong, getting direct hits on one large vessel and plastering the dock area. Two waves of 14 aeroplanes returned to Haiphong two days later on a sea search, again hitting shipping (including a large freighter) and the dock areas. 11 July saw three aeroplanes from the 375th BS attack an oil tanker in the bay off Haiphong, making individual runs but achieving only near misses. Two aircraft then went down and strafed the tanker from 75 ft. The other flight out that day – three aeroplanes from the 374th BS – managed to get a direct hit on a freighter in dock at Cam Pha port.

Over the next two weeks the group ran three more missions to the Haiphong area, attacking shipping, docks and the local cement plant. Then on 27 July the offensive shifted to a return to the Samah Bay area on Hainan Island. Fifteen aeroplanes reached the target area and scored hits on two freighters, but this time Japanese fighters rose to intercept. In a battle lasting 30 minutes the bombers claimed 14 fighters destroyed and six probably destroyed for no loss.

The 308th returned to Hong Kong on 19 July, with three waves of six aeroplanes each bombing the Taikoo ship yards, the navy yards and the docks at Kowloon. One aeroplane from the 373rd BS was lost on the return flight, running out of fuel 15 minutes from base. The pilot, Capt William Chenowith, ordered the crew to bail out and then tried to put the big bomber down in a rice paddy. Chenowith, his co-pilot and a Chinese co-pilot were killed in the attempt.

So far the B-24s had managed to avoid any losses to Japanese fighters on their unescorted missions, but this good fortune was not to last. Like their brethren in Burma, the JAAF fighter pilots in China were finding the Liberator to be a formidable opponent. Over the summer of 1943 the 25th and 33rd Sentais received advice on tactics to use against the B-24s

Maintenance at airfields in China was always a challenge. Here, a B-24 gets refuelled with hand pumps – an exhausting task (*RG 208-AA, Box 13: China-Air-Planes, NARA*)

from their colleagues in Burma – attack from the front quarter, go for the formation leaders and aim at the cockpit and the engines. That summer, too, the JAAF installed new warning radar which could detect incoming raids in time for the 'Oscars' to climb up to a favourable position from which to attack the bombers.

In mid-August the Japanese sent out several bombing raids and fighter sweeps against Fourteenth Air Force airfields in central China. Knowing that some of these missions had come from Hankow, Chennault planned a combined operation with the 308th BG's B-24s attacking the docks at Hankow, along the Yangtze River, while the B-25s of the 11th BS bombed Hankow airfield. P-40s would act as escorts.

The mission began at 0825 hrs on 21 August when 14 Liberators (seven each from the 374th and 375th BSs) took off from Chengkung and proceeded to a rendezvous with the B-25s and the P-40s over Hengyang. By an unfortunate coincidence the Japanese had sent out a fighter sweep to Hengyang shortly before the B-24s were due to arrive, drawing the P-40 escorts into a series of dogfights and preventing their rendezvous with the bombers.

The 308th BG's formation, lead by Maj Walter Beat from the 374th BS, passed to the west of Hengyang and proceeded on to Hankow unescorted. The bombers approached the target flying between 11,000 ft and 15,000 ft, but just before reaching Hankow the 'Oscars' of the 25th Sentai, which had been scrambled earlier, attacked the formation from head on. The unit's commander, ace Maj Toshio Sakagawa, led a flight of three Ki-43-IIs in a head-on attack against Maj Beat's aeroplane *Rum Runner*, knocking out two of the engines and setting the bomb-bay alight. Beat dived away from the 374th BS formation, the rest of the aeroplanes initially following him thinking he was taking evasive action. However, Beat's aeroplane was seen to blow up shortly thereafter.

Under heavy attack the 374th's formation was forced off its bomb run. The 375th managed to keep going with its run over the dock areas at Hankow. The gunners on the B-24s responded furiously as the 'Oscars' made repeated passes on the two formations for some 27 minutes, aggressively pressing home their attacks. Most of the passes were made from the '10' and '2 o'clock' positions, the fighters approaching both singly and in pairs from different positions, but aiming at the same aeroplane. Only *Je Reviens* from the 375th BS was lost. Seven members of the crew survived the crash landing, and with the help of Chinese guerrillas they made their way back to base. A third B-24 was so badly damaged that it had to land at an advanced field, while nine other bombers were also damaged in the fight.

The returning crews reported that they had been attacked by an estimated 60 fighters, and submitted claims for 57 confirmed and 13 probables – double the number of 'Oscars' (*text continues on page 61*)

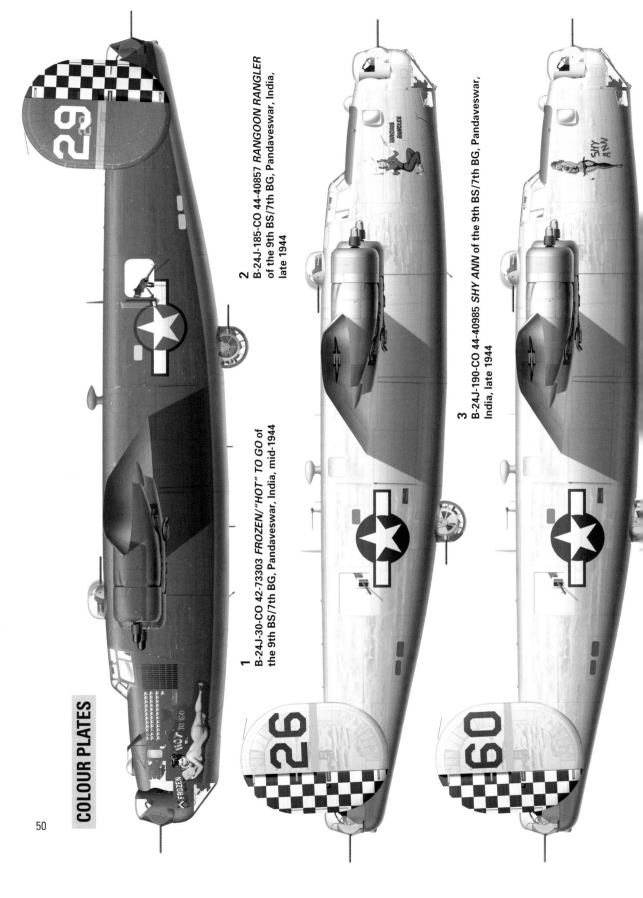

COLOUR PLATES

1
B-24J-30-CO 42-73303 *FROZEN/"HOT" TO GO* of the 9th BS/7th BG, Pandaveswar, India, mid-1944

2
B-24J-185-CO 44-40857 *RANGOON RANGLER* of the 9th BS/7th BG, Pandaveswar, India, late 1944

3
B-24J-190-CO 44-40985 *SHY ANN* of the 9th BS/7th BG, Pandaveswar, India, late 1944

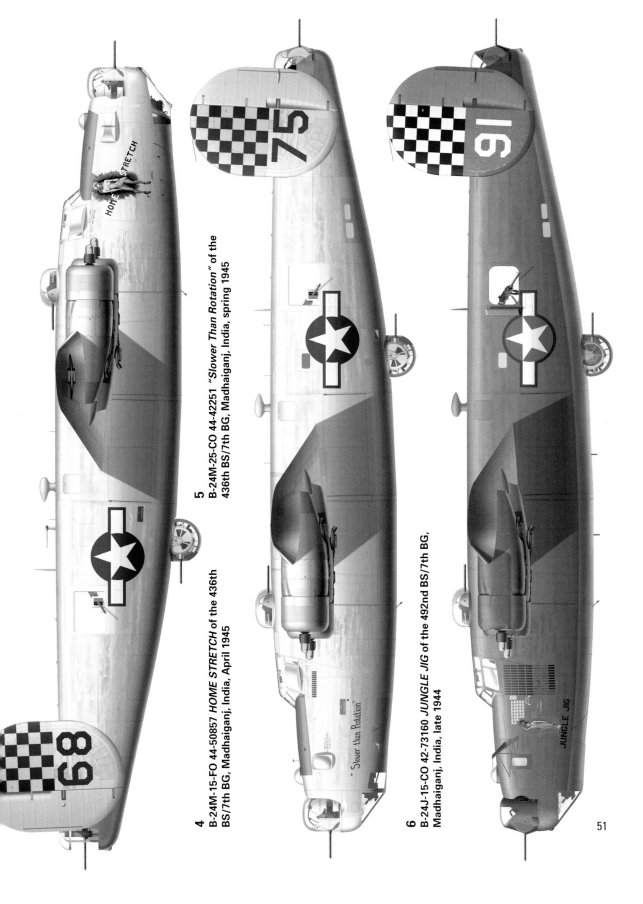

4
B-24M-15-FO 44-50857 *HOME STRETCH* of the 436th
BS/7th BG, Madhaiganj, India, April 1945

5
B-24M-25-CO 44-42251 *"Slower Than Rotation"* of the
436th BS/7th BG, Madhaiganj, India, spring 1945

6
B-24J-15-CO 42-73160 *JUNGLE JIG* of the 492nd BS/7th BG,
Madhaiganj, India, late 1944

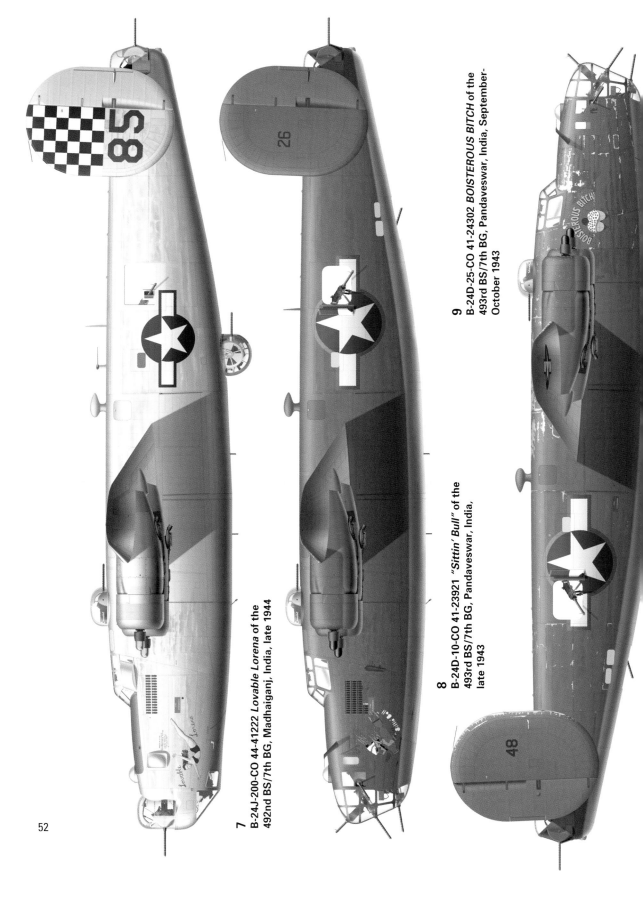

7
B-24J-200-CO 44-41222 *Lovable Lorena* of the
492nd BS/7th BG, Madhaiganj, India, late 1944

8
B-24D-10-CO 41-23921 *"Sittin' Bull"* of the
493rd BS/7th BG, Pandaveswar, India,
late 1943

9
B-24D-25-CO 41-24302 *BOISTEROUS BITCH* of the
493rd BS/7th BG, Pandaveswar, India, September-
October 1943

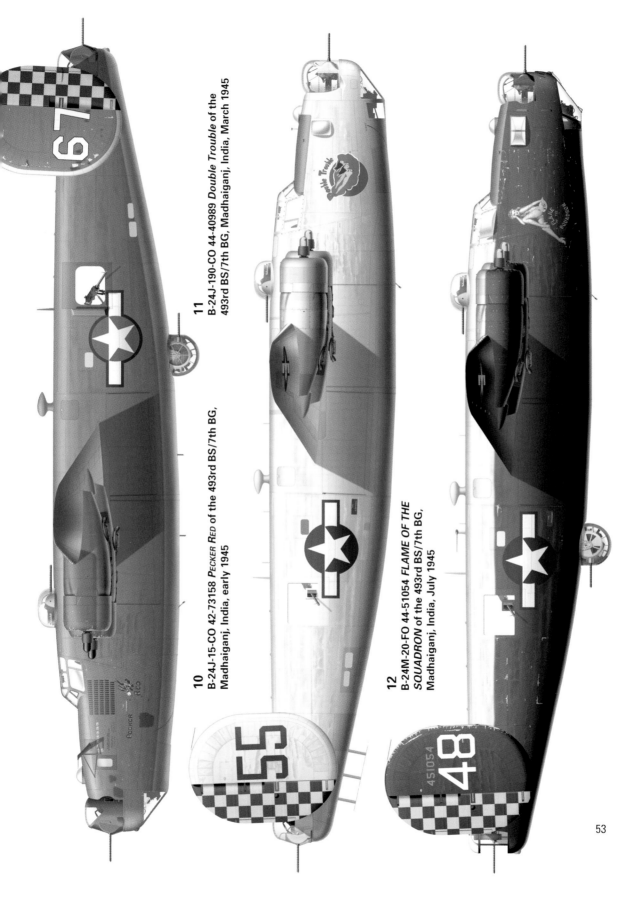

10
B-24J-15-CO 42-73158 *PECKER RED* of the 493rd BS/7th BG, Madhaiganj, India, early 1945

11
B-24J-190-CO 44-40989 *Double Trouble* of the 493rd BS/7th BG, Madhaiganj, India, March 1945

12
B-24M-20-FO 44-51054 *FLAME OF THE SQUADRON* of the 493rd BS/7th BG, Madhaiganj, India, July 1945

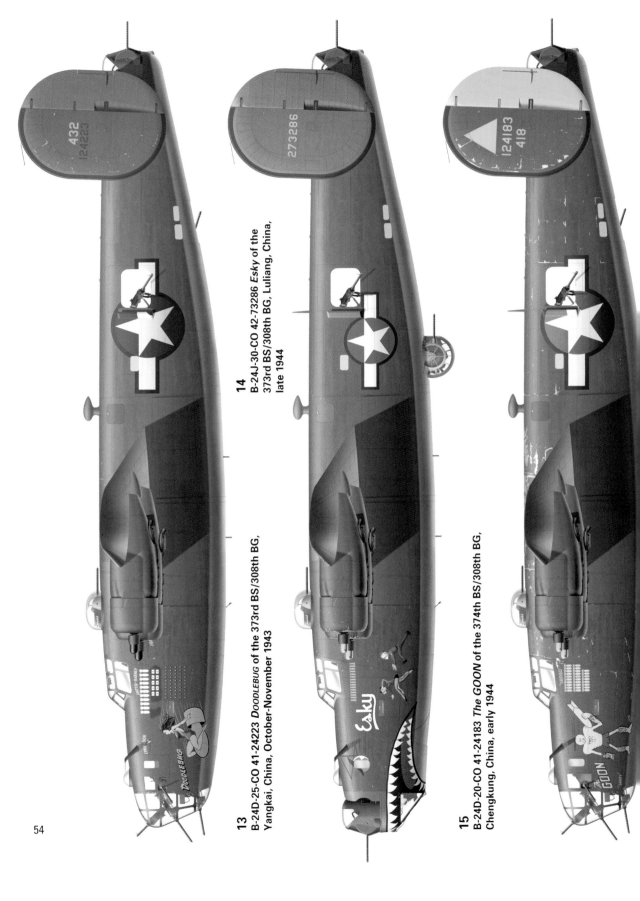

13
B-24D-25-CO 41-24223 *DOODLEBUG* of the 373rd BS/308th BG,
Yangkai, China, October-November 1943

14
B-24J-30-CO 42-73286 *Esky* of the
373rd BS/308th BG, Luliang, China,
late 1944

15
B-24D-20-CO 41-24183 *The GOON* of the 374th BS/308th BG,
Chengkung, China, early 1944

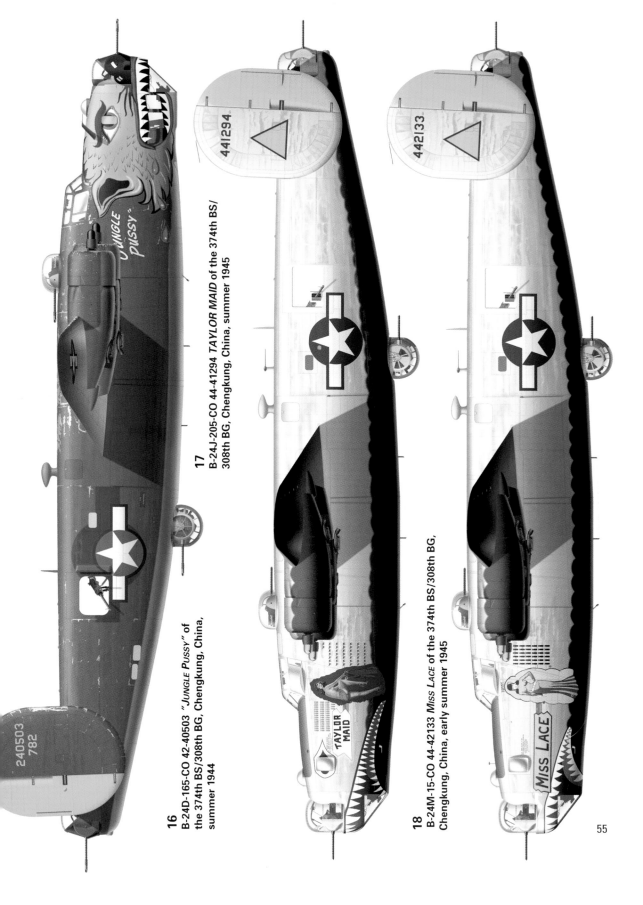

16
B-24D-165-CO 42-40503 "*Jungle Pussy*" of the 374th BS/308th BG, Chengkung, China, summer 1944

17
B-24J-205-CO 44-41294 *Taylor Maid* of the 374th BS/308th BG, Chengkung, China, summer 1945

18
B-24M-15-CO 44-42133 *Miss Lace* of the 374th BS/308th BG, Chengkung, China, early summer 1945

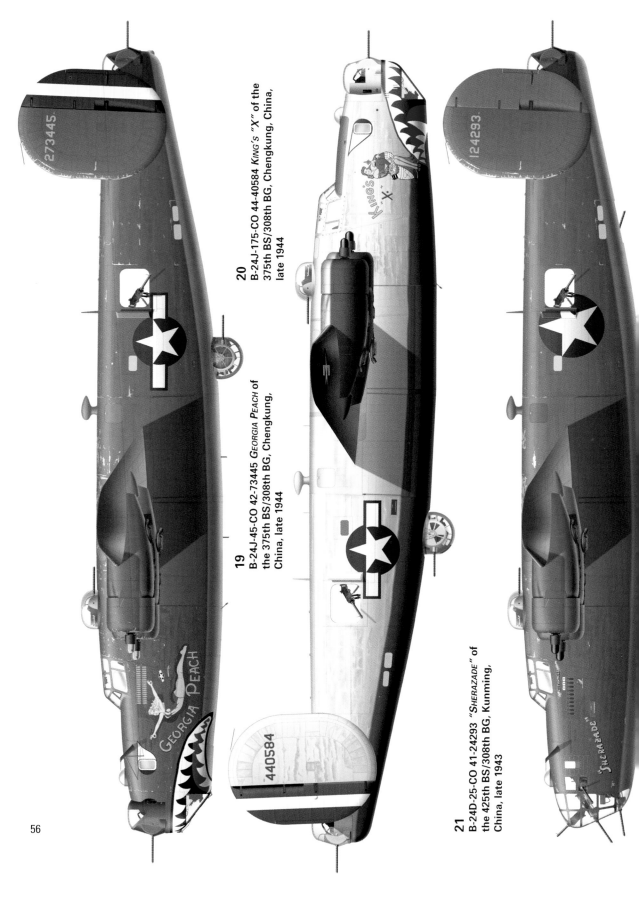

20
B-24J-175-CO 44-40584 *KING's "X"* of the
375th BS/308th BG, Chengkung, China,
late 1944

19
B-24J-45-CO 42-73445 *GEORGIA PEACH* of
the 375th BS/308th BG, Chengkung,
China, late 1944

21
B-24D-25-CO 41-24293 *"SHERAZADE"* of
the 425th BS/308th BG, Kunming,
China, late 1943

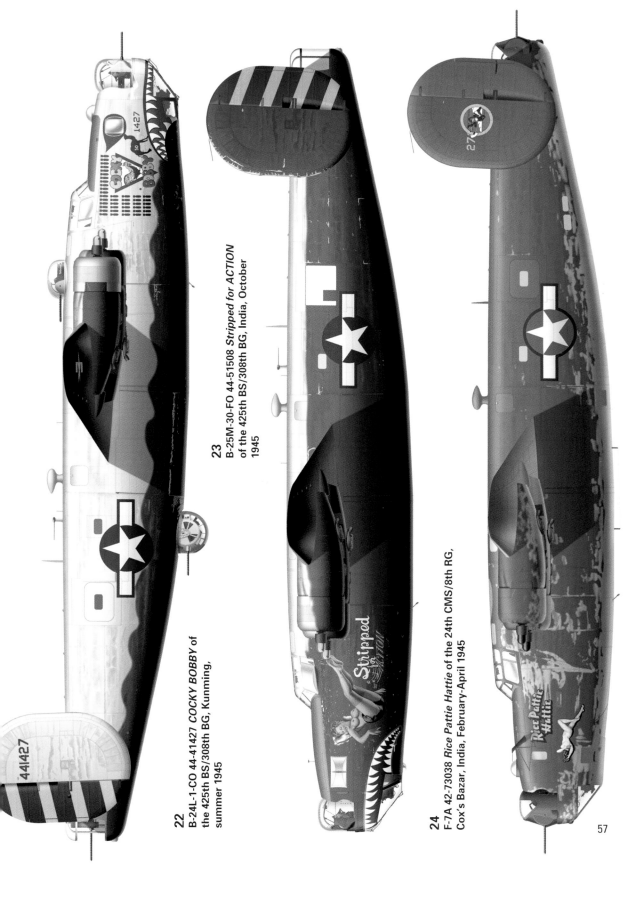

22
B-24L-1-CO 44-41427 *COCKY BOBBY* of
the 425th BS/308th BG, Kunming,
summer 1945

23
B-25M-30-FO 44-51508 *Stripped for ACTION*
of the 425th BS/308th BG, India, October
1945

24
F-7A 42-73038 *Rice Pattie Hattie* of the 24th CMS/8th RG,
Cox's Bazar, India, February-April 1945

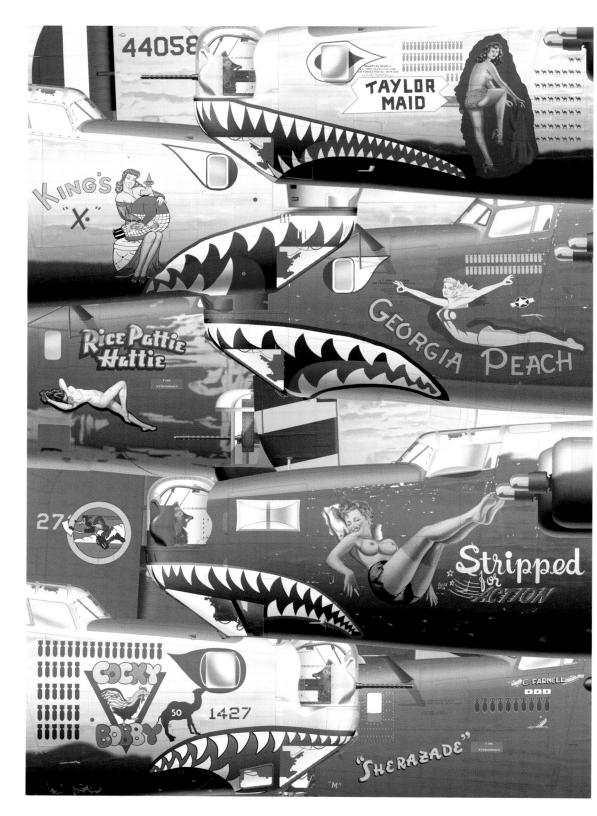

that had actually attacked, but an indication of the intensity of the air battle. SSgt Arthur Benko, flying in *The GOON* from the 374th BS, was given credit for five fighters destroyed and one damaged. The 25th Sentai suffered no losses, however.

Three days later it was the turn of the 373rd and 425th BSs to bomb Hankow, this time with the local airfield as the target for the combined force of B-24s and B-25s. Once again the mission was dogged with misfortune. On take-off the seven aeroplanes from the 373rd BS ran into bad weather and had to return to base. Maj H G Foster, leading the 425th BS's formation of seven aeroplanes in *"SHERAZADE"*, decided to continue with the target. The B-24s and B-25s rendezvoused at Hengyang, where an escort of P-38s and P-40s joined the bombers.

On the approach to Hankow some of the 425th aeroplanes mistook Wuchang airfield as the target and dropped their bombs prematurely, but the rest continued on and attacked the main base at Hankow. A few minutes after leaving the target the 425th BS and its six P-40 escorts ran into a hornet's nest – the 'Oscars' of the combined 25th and 33rd Sentais, some 40 fighters attacking seven bombers. According to the crews that returned from the mission, the Japanese fighters were 'better and faster' than any encountered previously, and 'the pilots were more aggressive'. Although Japanese accounts identify only the Ki-43-II-equipped 25th and 33rd Sentais as being involved in the action, these comments from the surviving 425th BS crews leave open the possibility that newly arrived Ki-44s of the 85th Sentai, which had recently been transferred to Hankow, may also have taken part in the interception.

The 425th was flying in two elements – one of three aircraft in the lead, with an element of four aeroplanes close behind. Lt Donald Kohsiek, co-pilot in *Sherazade*, later recalled 'I can still visualise the lines of "Zeroes" paralleling our course and peeling off, one at a time, to attack. They seemed to pass right over us'. An explosive round penetrated the cockpit, instantly killing Maj Foster and wounding Kohsiek. The battle went on for 45 minutes, the 'Oscars' knocking down four of the seven bombers. This time the fighters went after the wingmen more than the leaders of the formation. The left aeroplane in the lead element went down first, after which the fighters concentrated on the second element, sending three B-24s down one after another with their engines on fire and crewmen wounded. A number managed to bail out and make the long trek back to base with the help of the Chinese.

Gunners from the three bombers that made it back to base claimed 17 'Oscars' shot down and ten probables. In reality, the 25th Sentai had had one pilot killed, while the 33rd Sentai had lost two, including its Sentai commander. Tragically,

MISS CARRIAGE heads out on a mission over China during the summer of 1943 (*John V Osborne via the National Museum of the US Air Force*)

B-24D-25-CO 41-24293 *"SHERAZADE"*, which was named after the heroine of the film *Arabian Nights*. On 25 August 1943, Maj Horace Foster was killed while piloting this aeroplane during the 425th BS's disastrous mission to Hankow (*3A-01398, RG342FH, NARA*)

The nose glazing of B-24D-25-CO 41-24224 *THE MIGHTY EIGHTBALL* is covered up after the bomber had returned from a mission to Hainan. This aeroplane flew with the 373rd and later the 425th BSs, completing some 18 bombing missions and 75 'Hump' crossings. Sent back to the US in the spring of 1944, the B-24 was eventually lost on 29 June that same year when it flew into the side of a mountain near Tobe, Colorado, in poor weather during a navigation training exercise over the Rockies. All ten personnel aboard the aircraft were killed (*RG208-AA-Box 12: China-Air, NARA*)

425th BS B-24D-25-CO 41-24251 *CHUG-A-LUG* returns to Kunming after completing a mission in the late summer of 1943 (*RG208-AA, Box 108: Airplanes-Army-B-24-Exploits-China, NARA*)

on the return flight to Kunming the next day, one of the surviving 425th BS B-24s got lost in bad weather and crashed, killing all on board. In two missions the 308th BG had had 17 Liberators destroyed or badly damaged – a third of its strength.

Despite these losses the missions continued without let-up. On 26 August 15 B-24s went out to bomb the docks at Kowloon, six aircraft coming from the 373rd BS, seven from the 375th BS and two from the battered 425th BS. This time the fighter escort of P-38s and P-40s dealt with the Japanese fighters that rose to intercept the formation, the bombers' gunners claiming two destroyed and a probable from the few that managed to make passes on the 'heavies'. Then, on 31 August, the 373rd and 375th BSs sent 16 aircraft to bomb the Gia Lam airfield near Hanoi and the nearby Cobi barracks area. Nine aeroplanes from the 373rd hit the barracks while seven aircraft from the 375th bombed the airfield. The former was covered in cloud, but the 375th achieved an excellent pattern on the airfield. No enemy fighters came up to challenge the bombers. That same month the group received 14 new B-24Ds to make up for losses.

September proved to be another difficult month. The monsoon weather lingered on, allowing only two combat missions. Most of the time the squadrons undertook supply flights over the 'Hump' in an effort to build up the group's store of supplies, taking the opportunity to harass the Japanese by bombing towns in northern Burma with old Russian and Chinese bombs on the way to India!

French Indochina was again the target for the two combat missions. On 14 September the 373rd and 374th BSs flew unescorted to Haiphong to bomb the large cement plant and the dock areas. The 373rd had to turn back due to weather covering the target, but the 374th managed to hit the docks and several nearby ships. Six aircraft from the 373rd targeted the cement plant the next day too. One aeroplane turned back

CHUG-A-LUG **and two sister-ships head off on a mission over the rugged Chinese landscape in the late summer of 1943. Note that 41-24251 is the only Liberator with 'star-and-bar' national insignia (***RG208-AA, Box 108: Airplanes-Army-B-24-Exploits-China, NARA***)**

and the other five continued on to the target, again without fighter escort. Two days previously, the 25th and 33rd Sentais had flown a mission from nearby Gia Lam airfield, and unfortunately for the 373rd BS they were still there on the 15th. With ample warning of the approaching Liberators, 35 'Oscars' from the two *sentais* were in a favourable position to attack as the bomber formation turned onto its attack run. Coming in out of the sun from behind thunderheads, the fighters targeted the lead B-24 first then went after the other aeroplanes in the formation, making repeated passes mostly from the '10' and '2 o'clock' positions. Joe Mooney, top turret gunner in *Doodlebug*, flying in the low position, subsequently recalled;

'Capt Cunningham's aeroplane (*Daisy Mae*) was the first to get hit, and he winged over on fire. The formation seemed to split and the sky became choked with "Zeroes". We salvoed our bombs and tried to close up, but could not get close enough to help each other. All our guns were firing and my first hit was a "Zero" which had a gold-coloured band around the red meat ball on the fuselage. He was about 150 yards off when he blew up.'

The crew of *Doodlebug*, which was the only aeroplane to survive the mission, reported that the Japanese fighters were 'capable and aggressive'. The lead ship, *Daisy Mae*, pulled up after the attack, stalled, and went down in a spin. Then *Mohawk* fell away with two engines on fire, followed by a third B-24. *Doodlebug* and the other remaining unnamed bomber, flown by 2Lt Ruie Suggs, were harried for another 25 minutes as they flew in and out of clouds on the flight back to their base. Suggs' aeroplane may have been damaged or the crew wounded as it crashed just a few hundred yards short of the airfield at Kunming, killing the crew. *Doodlebug's* gunners submitted claims for ten fighters destroyed and 18 probables. For the second month in a row JAAF fighters had put one of the 308th's squadrons out of action. By now it was clear that the B-24s could fly unescorted missions only at their peril.

Chennault was determined to knock out the facilities in the Hanoi-Haiphong area that were providing support to the Japanese armies fighting in Burma and southwestern China. During October the 308th BG flew eight missions to Hanoi and Haiphong. On 1 October, 22 aeroplanes (seven from the 374th, seven from the 375th and eight from the 425th BSs) set off to bomb the docks, warehouses, and the main powerplant at Haiphong. This time the B-24s had an escort of P-40s. Seventeen aeroplanes hit their assigned targets with good results.

Shortly after dropping their bombs, the Liberators were intercepted by two groups of Japanese fighters from the 25th and possibly the 33rd Sentais. A smaller group of up to 12 fighters made several frontal assaults on the leading flights, but on this occasion they did not press home their attacks. A larger formation attacked from the rear, principally against the 374th BS's flight which was at the very rear of the formation. These attacks continued for 40 minutes, during which time the 374th's gunners claimed 21 fighters destroyed and three probables.

TSgt Arthur Benko in *The GOON* was given credit for seven fighters destroyed, bringing his score to 16 enemy aircraft and making him the leading ace in the Fourteenth Air Force. 'I never worked that turret so fast before', Benko said after the mission, during which he received slight wounds to his hand and neck. 'They tell me the scrap lasted about 40 minutes, but it seemed like a minute to me. You have to be on the alert every second. My guns jammed twice, and I had to clear them in a hurry.'

On 7 October ten B-24s, with P-40 and P-38 escorts, bombed the cement plant at Haiphong which provided 90 per cent of the cement for French Indochina with excellent results. Indeed, almost all the bombs salvoed fell directly on the target, putting the plant out of action for four months. After leaving the plant six to twelve enemy fighters attacked the formation, but the escorts kept them at bay, limiting the Japanese to only a few passes. The bomber gunners claimed three destroyed and eight more damaged. The next day nine B-24s returned to bomb Gia Lam airfield on the outskirts of Hanoi, again with a sizeable fighter escort. Excellent results were achieved once more. All subsequent daylight missions against targets in the Haiphong area were flown with escorts, allowing the B-24s to inflict serious damage on Haiphong's docks, nearby warehouses and other installations without interference from JAAF fighters.

In the 308th BG's first night mission, on 16 October, three

B-24D-20-CO 41-24183 *The GOON*, which flew with the 374th BS. TSgt Arthur Benko, seated beside his top turret, claimed 16 Japanese fighters shot down while flying in this aeroplane (*3A-01403, RG342FH, NARA*)

aircraft from the 425th BS mined Haiphong harbour while seven B-24s from the 375th BS bombed nearby Cat Bai airfield as a diversion.

That same month the 50th Sentai in Burma had sent detachments of fighters to airfields in northern Burma to attack transport aircraft flying the 'Hump' route. These missions, which the Japanese fighter pilots dubbed 'Tsujigiri' or 'street murder', were quite successful. The 50th shot down six transports and damaged several more. In response Chennault decided to use his B-24s as fighters. He ordered the 308th to send formations of bombers over the 'Hump' route in the hope of tricking the Japanese fighters into thinking that they were attacking formations of unarmed C-87s, the transport version of the B-24 then making regular runs along this route. The ruse worked.

On 27 October, six aircraft from the 374th BS flew from their base at Chengkung to Chabua, in India, flying a more southerly route than the transports to draw off the Japanese fighters. Eight enemy fighters attacked the formation, making mostly single head-on attacks for 50 minutes. The gunners claimed three fighters destroyed and one damaged. After refuelling at Chabua, five of the bombers made the return flight to Chengkung in the afternoon, again running into eight Ki-43-IIs from the 50th Sentai (only four 'Oscars' attacked). The gunners reported that these fighters were more aggressive, and they pressed their attacks to closer range, again making frontal attacks from the '10' and '2 o'clock' positions. The gunners claimed five destroyed, a probable and several damaged. Although the gunners claimed more aircraft than were actually shot down, for the 50th Sentai it was a costly mission. Three 'Oscars' were lost, with only one pilot rescued, at no cost to the B-24s.

The attacks on Japanese port facilities continued in November, with three missions to the Kowloon docks in Hong Kong. On 3 November 21 aircraft from all four squadrons of the group, with 30 P-40s and eight P-38s flying escort, went to Hong Kong, but they found the target covered by an overcast. After passing Canton on the way to the target, a flight of four to eight enemy fighters jumped the formation, followed by a second group reported to consist of about 30 fighters. The escorts immediately engaged the 'Oscars' and kept them away from the bombers.

At the same time heavy anti-aircraft fire came up, knocking out the No 1 engine of one of the three B-24s in the formation from the 425th BS. When this aeroplane dropped out of the formation it immediately came under attack by the Japanese fighters. Two Liberators from the 375th BS dropped back to offer protection until two P-40s arrived to provide cover. The gunners in these two bombers claimed one fighter destroyed, a probable and a damaged, while other gunners submitted claims for three more kills. The crew of the damaged 425th BS bomber finally had to bail out, all parachuting to safety. Chinese guerrillas quickly rounded up the crew and helped them work their way back to base.

The next attack was a combined night bombing and mine laying mission on 15 November by 20 aircraft from all four squadrons of the group. As a diversion, 14 aircraft would bomb the Kowloon docks while six aircraft from the 375th BS laid mines in the harbour. Weather prevented good bombing, although the mining operation was a success. On the return flight *The GOON* from the 374th BS ran into difficulties. When two engines went out, the pilot, Capt Sam Skousen asked the

308th BG B-24s form up over their base and prior to heading off on a mission over China during the autumn of 1943 (*3A-00959, RG342FH, NARA*)

flight engineer and the radio operator to stay with him, and ordered the rest of the crew to bail out. All but TSgt Arthur Benko and Lt Malcolm Sanders managed to reach friendly territory. Expecting to have to bail out at any moment, Skousen managed to get *The GOON* back to base after one of the dead engines started up again. Benko, the leading gunner ace of the Fourteenth Air Force, was later reported to have been killed by the Japanese.

As previously related, in November Maj Gen Stratemeyer had asked Chennault to lend the 308th BG to the Tenth Air Force for the series of combined missions against Rangoon. The 373rd and 374th BSs flew to Panagarh while the 375th and 425th BSs went to Pandaveswar to join the 7th BG. In India, the 308th's squadrons received brand new B-24Js, each unit getting nine of the newer model, while retaining three or four of the B-24Ds as a back-up for the Rangoon mission. The group returned 15 of the older B-24Ds to China, where they were used in ferrying missions over the 'Hump'. The plan was to have both groups fly to the same target on each mission, but each one would fly separately in its own formation, a few minutes behind the other.

The first mission on 25 November was aborted because of the weather, but on the 27th the 308th sent 28 B-24s to bomb the Insein locomotive works, flying behind the 7th BG's formation. Five aeroplanes had to turn back for various reasons, but the 23 that attacked managed to get all their bombs on the target area. While over Insein, four or five Ki-45s and five to 15 Ki-43-IIs intercepted the B-24s, and they continued to make attacks from all directions, concentrating on stragglers that dropped out of formation.

Although the crews did not consider the Japanese fighters to be particularly aggressive, they managed to knock down an aircraft from the 373rd BS and one from the 374th, flown by a new crew that had just joined the squadron a few days earlier. The 308th's gunners claimed one Ki-45 and five Ki-43-IIs shot down, with two Ki-45s and one Ki-43-II as probables.

The 308th sent out 27 B-24s the next day to bomb the Botataung dock area, 22 aircraft attacking the primary target with fair results despite it being covered in smoke from bombs dropped by the 7th BG, which had gone in first. A few enemy fighters made half-hearted attacks on the formation, one 'Oscar' being shot down and seen to crash.

The mission of 1 December saw the two groups flying in one large formation. Maj Paul O'Brien, CO of the 373rd BS, was leading the 308th's squadrons. Just before the start of the bomb run the JAAF

The rough Chinese airfields, mostly made by hand out of pressed and crushed rock, were hard on aeroplanes that were designed to operate from tarmac or concrete runways. This B-24 suffered a collapsed nose-gear on landing (*3A-02605, RG342FH, NARA*)

B-24D *floogie!* was photographed at Panagarh, India, in November 1943 (*7th BG(H) Historical Foundation, USAFA McDermott Library*)

fighters attacked the 7th BG, in the lead, downing several bombers before passing through to attack the 308th. The Japanese pilots were aggressive. They came barrelling in, concentrating their attacks on O'Brien's B-24 and hitting its No 1 engine, which began smoking. They also started a fire in the bomb-bay. O'Brien's aeroplane went into a steep dive down to the right, where it was seen to blow up. Nine other aeroplanes received varying degrees of damage, one B-24 being forced to land at Chittagong on the return flight. Following the 30-minute fight the group's gunners claimed six 'Oscars' destroyed.

The 308th's Indian sojourn ended with two night mining missions to Moulmein and the Rangoon estuary.

The 308th BG kept up a busy schedule during the last month of the year, flying nine bombing missions against rail facilities and airfields in China, French-Indochina and Thailand. The group flew two missions against the rail yards in Hanoi and two very successful unescorted missions into Thailand to bomb the rail yards at Chiang Mai and Lampang, which supported the Bangkok-Chiang Mai railway line.

Japanese airfields in China were the main target for the month, with two night missions being flown to the airfield at Hankow. On the night of 12 December an aircraft from the 373rd BS, having successfully bombed Hankow, had trouble finding a friendly airfield. The crew's experience gives an indication of the difficulties the B-24s often encountered flying over China. The navigator, Lt N J La Forest, recorded what happened on the return flight after bombing the target;

'We altered course to 220 degrees, flying to a dead reckoning position that put us on a heading of 270 degrees to Yangkai (the 373rd's base) or on a reciprocal course to Kweilin midway between the two stations. We continued on our course of 270 degrees to Yangkai, although the radio compass was fluctuating wildly, making it impossible for us to fly a sure radio course.

'Ten minutes beyond the expiration of our ETA, we turned on a heading of 180 degrees, hoping to find the lakes adjacent to Kunming from which we could establish a definite check point to come in on. All the while our radio operator was trying to gain a contact with ground stations, but apparently we had been issued with the wrong code sheet of the day, as the code names of the stations contacted did not jive with the frequencies on the sheet in our possession. After several hours of fruitless search we managed to obtain radio bearings from two stations we determined were Jorhat and Chabua from the coordinates they gave us. This fix placed us northwest of Kunming in the approaches to the "Hump". We then turned on a course of 172 degrees, which should have split the lakes at Kunming.

'After flying for the better part of an hour and not finding a field or check point, we decided the fix given to us must have been delayed too long, and therefore gave us an inaccurate position to start from. We then began circling again, attempting to establish contact with the ground, but every time we seemingly had a station within our grasp, the net would become jammed with static, music and jumbled voices. Eventually a clear, precise English voice contacted 836 and told us to fly a heading of 180 degrees.

'After 30 or 35 minutes on this course we decided among us that in all probability the heading given to us was put out by the Japs, and that we were heading into Jap-held territory, we then turned around on a reciprocal heading. At this point our fuel supply was dangerously low. We began looking for some flat country to bail out in. Lt Lacky (the pilot) managed to find a valley, and at approximately 0520 hrs ordered the first of the ship's crew to jump. He then circled the area until the remainder were gone, myself being the third from last to go.'

On this occasion the crew made it back to their base eight days later.

Two missions to bomb the Tien Ho airfield near Canton ran into Japanese fighters. Having learned their lesson, the bombers went in with fighter escort. On 23 December, 29 aircraft from all four squadrons set off for Tien Ho but the lead aeroplane mistook the nearby White Cloud airfield as the main target, so the entire formation went on to bomb White Cloud rather than break formation. The bombing was good, despite an interception by 15+ 'Oscars' probably from the 11th and 25th Sentais. They attacked for 20 minutes, although most were engaged in fights with the P-40 escorts. The bomber gunners claimed six destroyed, four probables and six damaged. Five B-24s were hit, one seriously.

The group sent another mission to Tien Ho the next day, and four aeroplanes from the 375th BS failed to contact the formation. Eighteen aircraft from the 373rd, 374th and 425th continued on, however, but due to a mistake on the approach to the main target they bombed a satellite airfield instead. This time some 25 fighters from the 11th, 25th, and 85th Sentais attacked the formation just before the bomb run, continuing their attacks for 25 minutes.

As usual, most attacks came from the front. The 25th Sentai's Capt Nakakazu, and his flight, attacked B-24D *Johnny Doughboy* of the 374th BS, setting it on fire. The aeroplane's right landing gear dropped down and the bomber peeled off to the left and fell into a spin. Five of the crew managed to bail out and had a miraculous escape. Landing only a few miles away from the airfield they had just bombed, they all managed to link up with Chinese guerrillas, who brought them to safety. Gunners from the 374th BS claimed seven fighters shot down, while the 373rd claimed ten confirmed, seven probables and six damaged, although it is unclear from Japanese records whether any fighters were lost.

Between its arrival in-theatre in March and the end of the year, the Liberators of the 308th BG had flown 51 combat missions over China and Southeast Asia, dropping 1196 tons of bombs and claiming 203 Japanese fighters destroyed for the loss of 29 B-24s and 124 men killed, missing in action or taken prisoner. In support of these combat missions the group's squadrons had flown 1331 round trips over the 'Hump', carrying 862,503 gallons of gasoline and 1,468,338 lbs of bombs and ammunition.

1944 would bring new missions and new challenges.

In late 1943 the 308th BG began to receive replacement aircraft equipped with a nose turret to improve the Liberator's forward armament. One such aircraft was *Nip Nipper,* a modified B-24D that flew with the 374th BS (*Eugene T Wozniak via Ken Easdon*)

SEA SEARCHES AND *ICHI-GO*

Japan's war economy was heavily dependent on imported raw materials to produce the equipment and supplies needed for its armed forces. Before the war, Japan imported 82 per cent of its petroleum, 75 per cent of its iron ore, 100 per cent of its bauxite, 100 per cent of its rubber and equally large percentages of critical chemicals. As an island nation, all these imports, and the finished products of industry – guns, tanks, ammunition, engines and spare parts – had to be transported to and from Japan by ship. This made the country's entire war effort vulnerable to attacks on shipping. As the United States Strategic Bombing Survey noted in its report on air operations in the CBI Theatre, 'A ship lost was thus felt in two ways – weakening the garrison for which it had been intended and weakening the war-making potential of the nation'.

Maj Gen Claire Chennault clearly understood this vulnerability. One of his main arguments for augmenting American air power in China had been the opportunity to increase attacks on Japanese shipping off the China coast, and when he finally had a heavy bomb group (and later a medium bomb group) assigned to the Fourteenth Air Force he ensured that shipping targets and port facilities would remain a high priority.

Indeed, during the autumn of 1943 the 308th BG targeted port facilities in Hong Kong and Haiphong, and from the beginning of 1944 it also began flying search missions over the South China Sea. A single squadron at a time went temporarily to the airfields at Kweilin and Liuchow, in eastern China, to conduct these flights whenever the weather was good, before returning home to Kunming after a few weeks. Using these bases in eastern China was important as it extended the range of the B-24s out over the South China Sea by two additional hours . The distance from Kunming to the China coast was more than 500 miles, but it was half that from Kweilin or Liuchow.

The sea search missions involved a change of tactics for the B-24 crews. The bombers went out in pairs during the day, usually flying parallel courses, to cover the sea routes to and from Japan in the South China Sea. If the Liberator crews found any ships they would

B-24J-35-CO 42-73320 *"ZOOT CHUTE"* was one of the new-build J-models issued to the 308th in November-December 1943. Assigned to the 373rd BS, it undertook numerous bombing missions and sea searches during the first half of 1944 (*3A-02189, RG342FH, NARA*)

bomb them from an altitude of 300 ft or less, before returning to strafe the ships if they could. Locating a vessel or a convoy was not easy, and enemy ships were often discovered purely by chance, especially in poor weather. Many times a ten-hour sea search mission would fail to find anything, with no alternative but to bring the bombs back to base. Because of the logistical problems associated with bringing supplies over the 'Hump', crews rarely jettisoned their bombs if they could get back to base without difficulty. For the first half of 1944, sea searches would outnumber regular bombing missions.

During the first half of January there were, however, three bombing missions that brought the 308th to new targets. On the 3rd, 28 B-24s from all four squadrons (escorted by two P-38s) flew a daylight mission against rail yards at Lampang, in northern Thailand. Then on 12 January eight B-24s from the 375th BS undertook a night mission to Takao, on the island of Formosa, to provide a diversion for three aircraft from the 373rd BS that were laying mines in the harbour. Six of the 375th's Liberators managed to locate and bomb an aluminium plant, which was the primary target. One aeroplane became lost and ran out of fuel on the return flight to Kweilin, but the crew managed to make it back to base two weeks later. That same night 17 aeroplanes from the 374th and 425th BSs flew a night mission to bomb the Bangsue marshalling yards near Bangkok, 14 aircraft managing to drop their bombs on the target.

In early January the 373rd BS had been chosen to carry out the first sea sweep assignment, flying to Kweilin and mounting its first mission on 10 January. Four days later two aeroplanes on a sweep of the sea lanes between Hainan Island and Luzon found two ships, one of which was a 300-ft freighter. The two bombers made five runs over the larger ship from different approaches but failed to score any direct hits. Both vessels were heavily strafed, leaving them smoking and the smaller one sinking. On 15 January two more aircraft went out, one returning after ten hours, having sighted nothing, while the second aeroplane simply disappeared.

Two subsequent sweeps also drew a blank, but on 20 January a pair of aircraft found two ships in the Formosa Straits, bombing and strafing both and leaving them sinking. During the attack return fire had hit one of the aeroplanes, jamming the front turret and wounding the co-pilot in the legs and pilot in the right hand and the left arm. The latter had been forced to drop the control wheel, sending the B-24 spiralling towards the sea. Despite his own wounds, co-pilot Lt Byron managed to grab control, right the aeroplane and fly it back to Kweilin.

Toward the end of January the 375th BS took over the sea sweep missions from Kweilin.

As a painful reminder that 'Hump' flights could be just as dangerous as combat missions, the

A B-24J from the 375th BS heads away from its target in southern China in early 1944 (*John V Osborne via the National Museum of the US Air Force*)

308th BG lost five aircraft on January 25 due to weather. They were on regular flights from Kunming and Chengkung to Chabua, in India, ferrying supplies back to China. The weather at Chabua had been reported as overcast, yet safe for flight, but when the aeroplanes arrived the airfield was completely socked in. Running out of fuel, one aeroplane crashed nearby, killing all but two of the crew. Two crews managed to bail out successfully and two aeroplanes were posted as missing.

February brought better results. Two aircraft from the 375th BS took off from Kweilin at 0645 hrs on 5 February for a sea search. Cruising over the sea lanes at 200 ft in poor weather, the two aircraft stumbled upon a convoy of nine to ten freighters, with a destroyer escort, east of Hong Kong. The crew of *Rose of Juarez* made three runs on the convoy. In the first of these the aircraft dropped three bombs on a freighter from an altitude of 100 ft, one bomb skipping into the side of the ship and exploding, causing the vessel to sink rapidly. The aircraft continued on its run, dropping three more bombs on a second ship and scoring one direct hit. This vessel was seen to explode, and it too sank quickly.

In the second aircraft the bombardier was unable to get the bomb-bay doors open fast enough due to the sudden appearance of the convoy, but it managed to damage one ship on the second run over the convoy and then score a direct hit on a vessel during the third run. This ship began settling in the water and the crew were seen to abandon it.

After several fruitless sea search missions, two aircraft from the 373rd BS and a pair from the 375th went out on 19 February. The B-24s from the 373rd BS came across two larger freighters with a destroyer escort

On 13 February 1944 the 308th flew a nearly perfect mission against the rail repair workshops at Vinh, in French Indochina. With the target clearly badly hit below, a B-24J of the 425th BS pulls away from Vinh. Note the bomber's newly introduced squadron tail markings, in this case yellow rudder stripes (*John V Osborne via the National Museum of the US Air Force*)

just off the northern tip of Formosa. While one bomber circled out of range, the first went in for a run on the larger of the two freighters, scoring two direct hits and setting this ship on fire. The second aircraft then came in, achieving one direct hit and a near miss on the second ship, which was also left smoking. Machine gun fire from the freighter hit the cockpit of the aeroplane on its approach, cutting the seat straps on the co-pilot's parachute. The arrival of the destroyer, which put up a heavy barrage of anti-aircraft fire, prevented a second run on the ships, but both freighters were deemed to have been sunk.

In between the sea search patrols the 308th BG flew several regular bombing missions and night mine-laying operations to Hong Kong and Takao. On 13 February 1944 the group flew a mission to bomb the rail repair workshops at Vinh, south of Haiphong in French Indochina, which was 'about as nearly perfect as any mission could be', according to the 308th's monthly history. Twenty-four aircraft from all four squadrons took off in the early afternoon without fighter escort for the flight to Vinh. One bomber aborted, but the remaining 23 flew on to Vinh in fine weather. With no fighter opposition and no anti-aircraft fire, the squadrons dropped down to between 6300-7000 ft for their bombing run, placing 95 per cent of their ordnance directly on target.

A lack of gasoline restricted flying operations during March. In fact, the group had insufficient fuel to send its own aeroplanes over the 'Hump' for more. Nevertheless, the 308th managed to send off nine sea searches, which sank no ships, but on two occasions managed to shoot down enemy flying boats.

On 19 March B-24D-80-CO 42-40622 *SWEEPY TIME GAL* (an aircraft from the 373rd BS that had been equipped with an early form of search radar) was flying a mission at 1500 ft off the southwest coast of Formosa when it picked up an enemy aircraft on its search radar. Soon the crew caught sight of a Kawanishi H6K5 Type 97 'Mavis' flying boat some six miles away. The Type 97 immediately headed for the clouds, with the B-24 in hot pursuit. Opening fire at long range, the crew saw some hits before losing the aircraft in more cloud.

Remarkably, one hour and 45 minutes later *SWEEPY TIME GAL* ran into a second Type 97 heading in its direction at the '10 o'clock' position. Like a true fighter pilot, Lt Glenn McConnell turned his bomber hard left and attacked the flying boat. The B-24 easily out-manoeuvred the lumbering Type 97, pulling into a position for the gunners to open fire. The Liberator's top turret gunner managed to get in several bursts that set the Type 97's No 3 engine on fire. The flames spread to the right wing, which then broke off, sending the Japanese flying boat crashing into the ocean.

The gunners on the Type 97 had fought back prior to their demise, however, hitting the B-24 in several places. A 7.7 mm shell penetrated the cockpit, knocking out both radio compasses, while a second shell cut the hydraulic line, sending a stream of fluid into the bomb-bay and knocking out the aeroplane's electrical equipment. A third shell started an oil leak in the No 3 engine. The return fire also wounded three of the crew. Once the 'Mavis' had been despatched, two of the gunners went into the bomb-bay, cranked open the bomb-bay doors and then manually salvoed the bombs. *SWEEPY TIME GAL* made it back to Kweilin.

Two days later another pair of bombers (from the 374th and 425th BSs) on a sea search mission off the southwest coast of Formosa ran into another Type 97. The two B-24s made three passes, shooting the 'Mavis' into the ocean, but once again the Japanese gunners had managed to badly damage one of the Liberators.

The 308th had begun using B-24s with search radar in March, referring to them as 'sniffers'. These aeroplanes, which had a better chance of locating shipping in adverse weather, would often go out in pairs or as part of a pair with a standard J-model. More radar-equipped aircraft arrived during March 1944, allowing additional 'sniffer' sea searches to be made during April. And this month, the 'sniffers' really came into their own, sinking one ship on 2 April and two more five days later. However, on the latter date one of the highly prized 'sniffer' aircraft had to be abandoned when its crew was unable to locate Kweilin in bad weather on the return leg of their mission.

On 18 April *SWEEPY TIME GAL* and another 'sniffer' aircraft took off on a sea search mission. The second aeroplane returned safely, but 42-40622 was shot down in the Lyemun Gap channel to the east of Hong Kong Island, crash-landing in the water. Lt Glenn McConnell and one of his gunners managed to escape from the wreckage to become PoWs, but the rest of the crew perished. The Japanese later raised the wreck of the aeroplane and put it on display in Hong Kong.

In terms of damage to Japanese shipping, the mission of 22 April was one of the best single operations in the group's history. The Fourteenth Air Force had received intelligence about a Japanese convoy harbouring at Cape St Jacques that was preparing to go up-river to Saigon. Seven aircraft (three from the 374th BS and four from the 425th BS) flew to Liuchow, one of Chennault's east China airfields located south of Kweilin, on the 21st, and the next day took off before noon to arrive over the target area in the evening so that the return flight would be made in darkness.

The seven aircraft flew through atrocious weather across the Gulf of Tonkin and down the coast of French Indochina, one B-24 turning back after it was unable to break through a severe front. The remaining six bombers reached Cape St Jacques and proceeded to make individual attacks from low level. The Japanese were taken by surprise, which meant that the first Liberators encountered no anti-aircraft fire. Six ships were attacked and sunk, including three tankers and a small naval vessel. B-24 *CHUG-A-LUG III* had its hydraulics shot out, which meant that it landed with no flaps and only one main landing gear locked down.

To date the Liberators had claimed eight ships sunk and more damaged for the loss of only two aircraft, one to enemy action and one to fuel exhaustion. During

A wartime Japanese photograph of the wreckage of B-24D-80-CO 42-40622 *SWEEPY TIME GAL* on the docks at Hong Kong after having been shot down on 18 April 1944. The Japanese raised the bomber from Hong Kong harbour, where it had crash-landed (*Author's collection*)

73

May this ratio would shift dramatically. The month began with a successful sea search mission on the 3rd, an aircraft from the 373rd BS encountering a small six-ship convoy off the China coast. Flying through heavy weather with a low overcast, the aeroplane made two runs against the largest freighter in the convoy, scoring two direct hits. The ship was seen to sink a few minutes later. A 374th BS aeroplane found a smaller freighter a short while later, and in three separate runs it left the ship listing heavily.

On 6 May these same two crews came across another convoy, but this time with an escort of three destroyers and a gun boat, which immediately put up a heavy barrage of anti-aircraft fire. The two bombers climbed and then made five runs over the convoy at 7500 ft, possibly damaging one larger freighter. Sea searches on 10, 11 and 12 May came up empty, but on the 19th two B-24s (one from the 374th, flown by 2Lt Grady Walton, and one from the 425th, flown by Lt Glenn Lowe) came across a small convoy of four freighters and a destroyer east of Hong Kong. Lowe, flying *Burma Queen*, made a run on a large 400-ft freighter, dropping three 500-lb bombs close to the ship.

As he circled for his second run, Lowe saw Walton's B-24 also manoeuvring to attack the convoy. Lowe came in and dropped his remaining bombs, scoring several near misses and leaving the aft end of the freighter smoking. Walton then made his approach on the same ship. The vessel sent up a stream of anti-aircraft fire, hitting Walton's B-24 in both wings and setting them on fire. The big bomber passed over the freighter, glided down into the water, skipped, hit again and exploded.

The next day the 308th BG suffered its worst losses since the mission to Haiphong the previous September. Early in the morning of 20 May a B-24 on a search mission out of Kweilin came across a ten-ship convoy and radioed its position. Thirteen B-24s (four from the 373rd, one from the 374th, three from the 375th and five from the 425th) that had been temporarily based at the airfield at Liuchow in preparation for another mission, were hastily sent off one at a time to attack the convoy.

One aircraft had to turn back, and a second reached the target area but failed to locate the convoy. It appears that the remaining 11 B-24s, attacking separately, possibly attacked two different convoys, both of which had destroyers as escorts. The destroyers and the freighters put up an intense barrage as each bomber attacked. Returning crews reported seeing one Liberator attack a destroyer, burst into flames and crash into the sea just after its attack, which also left the vessel ablaze. A second bomber attacking the same convoy was also hit hard, leaving the scene smoking before it too crashed into the sea on fire. A third B-24, attacking what was possibly the second convoy, exploded in mid-air.

Two of these aeroplanes were from the 373rd and one from the 425th. All three had been carrying bomb-bay tanks, which may have contributed to the aeroplanes going down in flames. Two other bombers, one from the 375th and one from the 425th, were so badly shot up during their attacks that both crews bailed out once they were back over land.

B-24J-35-CO 42-73319 *The BITCH'S SISTER* **was a sister-ship to** *"ZOOT CHUTE"*, **it too having been issued to the 375th BS in India for the November 1943 Rangoon raids. The bomber flew on two of these missions, and survived the costly 20 May 1944 sea search operation that saw the 308th BG lose five B-24s** (*Vern P Martin*)

Five aircraft and three crews had been lost for a score of one destroyer probably sunk, one large freighter probably sunk, three small vessels sunk and three freighters damaged.

LAB BOMBERS

The sea search missions flown in April and May demonstrate the difficulties the 308th BG encountered in trying to attack Japanese shipping effectively. Even in good weather finding ships in the area of the South China Sea was always a challenge – in poor weather the task was even greater. Flying a gruelling ten-hour mission without result was hard on the air crews and aeroplanes, not to mention a waste of gasoline carried over the 'Hump' with such effort. Furthermore, attacking a heavily armed convoy in broad daylight in a B-24 was no picnic, as the 20 May mission clearly showed.

It appears that as the Fourteenth Air Force's attacks on shipping by its heavy and medium bombers increased, the Japanese responded by arming their merchant vessels and allocating more escorts to convoy duty. The partial answer to the challenges of locating shipping and defensive fire came with the introduction of special B-24s equipped with the Low-Altitude Bombing (LAB) system.

The latter came out of a need to link ASV radar, which could locate shipping at night and in bad weather, with an automatic bomb release system that would allow accurate blind bombing to take place at low altitudes. The AN/APQ-5 system that was developed to meet this requirement linked the SCR-717 microwave search radar with the Norden bombsight. The search radar could locate a target 30+ miles away from the aircraft. The radar operator's job was to pick up the target on the ASV system and direct the pilot to it. When in range, the bombardier selected the target on the AN/APQ-5 indicator, which had its own radar scope, and took over the approach with the call of 'PDI on' over the intercom. The bombardier guided the pilot on the bomb run to the target, keeping it within the cross-hairs on his radar scope. The LAB system calculated the correct release point and, using radar returns from the target, released the bombs automatically (usually three bombs a run).

With a trained crew – pilot, radar operator and bombardier – working in close coordination, the LAB system could achieve excellent results. Attacking at night preserved the element of surprise, and avoided, at least in the initial attack, defensive anti-aircraft fire from convoy escorts. Often, the first indication a ship would have that it was under attack was the bomb bursting alongside or on the ship itself.

In the autumn of 1943 a unit of LAB-equipped Liberators, referred to unofficially as 'SB-24s' or more colloquially as 'snoopers', was sent to Guadalcanal for service with the Thirteenth Air Force and immediately started enjoying remarkable results. A second unit went out to join the Fifth Air Force in New Guinea. Based on this success, the USAAF sent a special LAB force (commanded by Lt Col William D Hopson) to the Fourteenth Air Force to aid the anti-shipping campaign.

One of the LAB-equipped Liberators issued to the 308th BG in the spring of 1944, B-24J-65-CO 42-100036 *"TENNESSEE BELLE"* arrived in China in May of that year. Lt Jaye LeVan was flying this aircraft when he and his crew claimed a Japanese cruiser sunk on 19 August 1944 (*Jim Augustus*)

In April 1944 Hopson led the first section of 20 trained crews in brand new B-24Js equipped with the LAB system to China to begin operations. On arrival, the crews were distributed among the 308th BG's four squadrons. As a general practice, the group attempted to keep eight operational LAB aircraft at Kweilin, two from each squadron, rotating aircraft back for maintenance as needed. As one of these crews recalled, 'the list of obstacles we faced was formidable: single-aeroplane missions at maximum range from base; minimal aids to navigation and scant information on weather; complete dependence on newly-developed and still unreliable electronic equipment; minimal logistical support, particularly for the electronic equipment; operation from bases which were under attack by land and air; and an initially sceptical command and general staff structure'.

The first 'snooper' mission with the new LAB aircraft on 24 May to Samah Bay on Hainan Island was aborted due to technical problems, but the next night two 'snooper' aircraft went back to the Samah Bay area. One Liberator made a run at 1000 ft on a 200-ft freighter, scoring three direct hits, while the second aircraft bombed a 300-ft freighter from 2000 ft and also scored direct hits, sinking both ships.

The plan for the following night was to have one 'snooper' aircraft bomb the dock area at Samah Bay to drive shipping out into the outer harbour, where other 'snooper' aircraft would be waiting. The first aircraft, assigned to the 374th BS, failed to return from the mission (this was the first LAB aeroplane lost by the group), while a second B-24 had to abort when its radar failed. The third bomber ended up attacking a small island by mistake, as it looked like a ship on the radar returns!

On 27 May two more 'snoopers' went out on a mission but failed to find any shipping. One aircraft was ordered to proceed to the airfield at Lungling when weather closed the runway at Kweilin. The next morning, the crew took off from Lungling to return to their base, but the aircraft crashed into a nearby mountain in poor weather and all on board were killed. Two LAB crews had been lost in three days of operations. On 29 May, in the last 'snooper' mission of the month, one aircraft located and sank a 250-ft freighter off Hainan Island.

During June, however, the LAB bombers really came into their own. They claimed 16 ships sunk totalling 53,100 tons, five probably sunk and ten damaged for the loss of three aircraft and one crew – an impressive performance given the often very poor weather off the coast at this time of year. The LAB B-24s flew 71 sea search sorties that month and managed to sink ships on 11 nights. A sea search mission on 8 June 1944, described in the 308th BG official history, gives a flavour of what these sorties were like;

'Plane No 275, Lt Wallace's crew, on LAB picked up a ship from 35 miles away. Using LAB equipment, they closed on the ship through a turbulent series of storms. They had a "dry run" on the ship and then, on a course of 160 degrees, and at 30 degrees to the length of the ship, bombed, dropping all eight bombs in train at intervals of 50 ft. The ship disappeared two-and-a-half minutes after bombing and another run was then made over the same point. Nothing seen in the scope. Immediately following the bombing run three distinct flashes were seen to the rear of the aeroplane through the undercast. This ship is claimed as sunk.'

The LAB bombers flew regular searches over the South China Sea, the Formosa Straits, the area around Hainan Island and off the coast of Shanghai. The group also began flying sweeps down the Yangtze River to disrupt the extensive river traffic along this vitally important communications route. While several ships were hit and sunk, the multiplicity of small and medium sized ships along the river made target selection difficult. Weather and shortages of fuel during July and August hindered operational flying, but the sea search missions continued whenever possible.

On a sea search mission on 19 August Lt Jaye LeVan and his crew came across an Imperial Japanese Navy cruiser, making three runs on the ship during the course of one hour and 48 minutes, leaving it sinking.

B-24J-180-CO 44-40832 *Miss Beryl* was a late-model LAB-equipped Liberator that was assigned to the 374th BS in August 1944 and flew sea search and regular bombing missions until April 1945 (*John V Osborne via the National Museum of the US Air Force*)

From the first LAB mission on 25 May until the end of August, the LAB bombers had flown 134 sorties, located 391 Japanese ships, attacked 147 and claimed 34 merchant ships and two naval vessels sunk, seven probably sunk and 17 damaged for the loss of seven aircraft. These missions were but a prelude to an exceptional performance during the month of September. After three months of intensive flying the LAB crews had built up extensive experience with their equipment and their tactics. Luck and skill had also enabled several pilots and bombardiers to run their scores of Japanese ships sunk or damaged into double-digit figures.

By the early autumn the 308th BG had also acquired more LAB-equipped Liberators. Indeed, during the month of September the group had an average of 24 LAB and 14 regular B-24s in commission. That month the LAB bombers submitted claims for 32 merchant ships sunk totalling 104,000 tons, two naval vessels sunk and another eight merchant and naval ships probably sunk or damaged. These results gave the 308th its best month ever in terms of ships sunk, with a remarkable 70 per cent of the vessels attacked being destroyed.

On one mission on 19 September, two LAB aircraft set off from Liuchow in the late afternoon to attack a convoy in the Formosa Strait that night. The first aeroplane claimed two freighters sunk and one damaged, while the second, after intercepting a message reporting the convoy from the first LAB ship, flew to the area and made five runs. It scored direct hits on two tankers and two freighters, claiming all four as sunk when the blips disappeared from the radar scope.

Weather was an ever-present problem when operating in the South China Sea, and it was at its worst during the monsoon season from June through to September. Elmer Haynes, who flew as a co-pilot in the 375th BS, recorded his experiences with the weather on one September mission in the book *Chennault's Secret Weapon*, based on his diaries and notes:

The BITCH'S SISTER leads a flight of B-24s from the 375th BS away from the target in mid 1944 (John V Osborne via the National Museum of the US Air Force)

Maj Horace Carswell was posthumously awarded the Medal of Honor for his actions on the night of 26 October 1944. A former flight instructor and operations officer, he had been assigned to the 308th BS in April 1944. Because of his flying experience Carswell often flew with different crews to observe them in combat (RG111SC-313635-NFS, NARA)

'We were called to the briefing room at 2000 hrs, received reports of a five-ship convoy, and took off at 2130 hrs. We would be flying into a heavy weather front, with towering cumulus thunderheads along the squall line. Air turbulence would be strong. Under normal conditions, a pilot would never dream of flying an aeroplane of this size through this kind of weather system. It was impossible to know what to expect in the wake of violent and tumultuous wind, rain, and lightning. But if we could cross the front in one piece, the cooling night air would dissipate the storm clouds by the time we had completed the mission and were heading back to Liuchow.

'As we entered the squall line, the crew were alerted to tie everything down and secure themselves for a rough ride. Milt (the pilot) and I tried to keep the wings level and the altitude steady. Nothing else could be done except pray, and hope that our B-24 would hold together and not flip over onto its back. An aeroplane could be ripped to pieces in the rampaging storms of a thunderhead, with its vicious, wind-shearing currents acting like giant scissors on the body and wings of an aircraft. The stress on an aeroplane traversing a weather system of this kind was so great that rivets would pop, warping the fuselage. Many B-24s were so badly mangled that once safely on the ground they never flew again.'

Although subsequent months could not match the September record, the LAB bombers maintained their attacks on Japanese shipping well into 1945, sinking six to 14 ships a month and damaging many more.

For his heroic actions on a sea search mission on 26 October 1944, Maj Horace Carswell was awarded a posthumous Congressional Medal of Honor, the only airman in the CBI Theatre to be so honored. He and his crew had attacked a Japanese convoy, scoring a near miss against a destroyer. Knowing that the convoy was now fully alert, Carswell nevertheless decided to make a second run, getting two direct hits on a large tanker, but the anti-aircraft fire knocked out two of his engines and damaged a third, wounded his co-pilot and ripping through the bombardier's parachute. Once over land, and with the third engine faltering, Carswell ordered the rest of the crew to bail out while he stayed with his co-pilot and bombardier in the hope of making a crash-landing, only to lose his life when his aeroplane flew into a mountain.

THE *ICHI-GO* OPERATION

The anti-shipping campaign had been an unparalleled success, but this very success had provoked – as Gen Stilwell had feared – a violent Japanese reaction. In April 1944, the Japanese Army had launched the *Ichi-Go* offensive with the objective of expanding their control over eastern China. Chennault began to lose his airfields one by one as the Chinese armies proved helpless in the face of the Japanese onslaught.

Ichi-Go had several objectives. With the success of the Fourteenth Air Force's attacks on Japanese land communications within China and shipping off the coast, and the JAAF's failure to prevent these attacks, the Japanese Army command in China decided that the only alternative was to destroy the Fourteenth Air Force's forward airfields through a ground offensive. At the same time, the Japanese hoped to capture a rail corridor that would extend from Peiping in the north all the way to French Indochina. This would, in theory, reduce the impact of the anti-shipping campaign on the flow of supplies to and from Japan.

Ichi-Go lasted from April to December 1944. In the first phase of the operation the Japanese Army captured the railway line between Kaifeng, on the Yellow River, and Hankow, on the Yangtze River. The second phase of the operation commenced in May when Japanese armies began advancing south from Hankow, capturing Changsha, Hengyang, Kweilin and Liuchow over the next several months with the assistance of Japanese Army units attacking out of Canton. By December 1944 the Japanese had successfully established a rail corridor to French Indochina and had eliminated many of Chennault's forward bases in eastern China.

The Fourteenth Air Force struggled to provide support to the Chinese armies. The main burden fell on the fighters and medium bombers,

The 308th BG attacked Hong Kong on 16 October 1944, with the Kowloon docks being particularly badly hit as this photograph shows. Decades later, a Chinese woman, now living in Seattle, Washington, recalled how beautiful the formation looked as it made its stately way overhead with the sun glinting off the silver-coloured fuselages against a blue sky (*3A-02644, RG342H, NARA*)

which flew countless missions, to the extent that gasoline supplies allowed, against the steadily advancing Japanese offensive. The heavy bombers of the 308th BG were regularly called on to target Japanese military installations, supply areas and rail yards in an attempt to disrupt the flow of supplies to the enemy in the field. Operations in support of the Chinese armies began in late April with two abortive missions to bomb bridges across the Yellow River.

During May the Liberators concentrated on targets in southwest China to support the Chinese army's offensive in northern Burma, but in June they returned to bombing military installations and storage areas in central and eastern China in a series of day and night attacks. On 15 June 23 aircraft from all four squadrons made a night attack on a warehouse area near Canton, although haze prevented accurate bombing. The group then started using the LAB-equipped B-24s as pathfinders during night attacks. On a mission to bomb warehouses and storage areas at Yochow, north of Changsha, on 18 June, a LAB bomber went in first to mark the target area with incendiaries, after which 12 aircraft bombed individually at altitudes from 2800 ft up to 7000 ft.

Six nights later the group scheduled a mission to target the docks and shipping at Hankow, this time sending in four LAB aircraft as pathfinders. They picked up the target area on their search radar, and although the numerous small lakes and streams in the area made it difficult to

A B-24J from the 425th BS completes its bombing run on a military storage depot at Sinshih on 8 July 1944. Aircraft from the 373rd and 375th BSs can just be made out in the upper left corner of this photograph, the units commencing their bombing runs (3A-02716, RG342H, NARA)

These two 308th BG B-24s were sent bridge-busting in French Indochina in September 1944 (3A-02771, RG342H, NARA)

identify, they managed to mark the docks with their incendiaries for the follow-on bombing by 14 aeroplanes. One Liberator failed to return from the mission. The 308th BG attacked Hankow again on the night of 26 June using the same procedure. The four LAB bombers lit up the target, then six out of the ten aeroplanes that reached the target bombed individually, getting 80 per cent of their ordnance in the right area.

In addition to these bombing sorties, the group increased the number of mining missions flown to the Hong Kong-Canton and Yangtze River areas to slow the flow of supplies to Japanese forces.

With the fighters preoccupied flying close support missions and escorting the medium bombers, the 308th BG conducted mostly night bombing operations during July and early August, continuing to use the technique of sending in LAB bombers to mark the target area with incendiaries for the following aircraft. With the primitive field facilities available, wrestling a heavily laden B-24 into the air at night was one hell of a challenge. On one such mission to bomb the airfield at Paluichi, two aircraft (one from the 374th and one from the 375th) crashed on take-off from Chengkung. Only four crew members survived.

The few day operations that were undertaken all had fighter escorts, and they did an excellent job of fending off intercepting fighters on a return mission to Yochow on 25 July as well as during an attack on

In mid-July the 308th BG made a series of attacks on Changsha in support of Chinese troops fighting against the *Ichi-Go* offensive (*3A-02631, RG342H, NARA*)

During 1944 most of the 308th BG's day missions had a fighter escort. Here, B-24J-35-CO 42-73318 *Karachi Kourier* flies wing on B-24J-25-CO 42-73253 *Burma Queen* – both long-serving aircraft with the 425th BS – on a mission to counter the *Ichi-Go* offensive in early summer 1944 (*3A-00957, RG342FH, NARA*)

On 3 August 1944, 23 aircraft bombed the railway yards at Yochow, getting 90 per cent of their bombs in the target area. Gunners shot down one fighter (*3A-00958, RG342H, NARA*)

B-24J-170-CO 44-40584 *King's X* from the 375th BS pulls away after bombing Hengyang on 16 September 1944 after its fall to the advancing Japanese (*3A-02641, NARA*)

Samah Bay four days later. Although few Japanese fighters managed to penetrate the escort screen, the bomber gunners claimed three fighters destroyed on these two missions.

The 308th ran into Japanese fighters once again on two day missions to bomb the rail yards at Yochow in August. On the 3rd, 23 aeroplanes, with an escort of P-40s, bombed the yards from 16,000 ft with excellent results, getting 90 per cent of their ordnance into the narrow target area. Immediately after the bomb run 12 to 15 'Oscars' attacked the formation. The lead Liberator squadron took the brunt of the attack, with the Ki-43-IIs making a number of frontal passes. None of the attacks were

Re-supply flights over the 'Hump' continued throughout 1944. Here, the 374th BS's B-24J-25-CO 42-73257 *80 Days*, named for the time it took to get to China from the States, flies over the rugged terrain of the 'Hump' route. The aircraft was lost over China on 30 October (*3A-01019, RG342H, NARA*)

considered particularly aggressive. The gunners claimed one fighter destroyed, a probable, and three damaged.

The group sent 24 aircraft to Yochow at the end of the month, and on this occasion the 'Oscars' were out in force. Some 20 to 30 fighters hit the formation five minutes before starting its bomb run, and they continued their attacks for 30 minutes. These fighters were very aggressive, pressing home their attacks despite the escorting P-40s and P-51s doing their best to keep the JAAF interceptors at bay. Seven of the bombers were damaged, one severely. The pilot of the latter machine made a successful crash-landing with no nose wheel and a wing tank on fire. The gunners claimed 11 fighters confirmed, one probable and two damaged in their biggest air battle in months.

The pace of operations against the *Ichi-Go* offensive left the Fourteenth Air Force desperate for fuel and other supplies that could not be completely made up through ATC flights over the 'Hump'. Chennault managed to get the 7th BG shifted to flying gasoline to China during the monsoon season in India.

The 308th BG continued to fly regular supply flights over the 'Hump', but the group devoted an

Taking off in an over-loaded B-24 from a rough Chinese airfield often led to disaster. This 425th BS Liberator crashed at the start of a mission on 8 July 1944. Miraculously, one crewman survived this complete wreck with only slight injuries (*3A-02593, RG342H, NARA*)

Miss Beryl participated in the large-scale mission to Hankow on 18 December 1944, when the 308th BG sortied 30 B-24s. Twentieth Air Force B-29s also took part in the operation, leaving the city's waterfront area ablaze (*3A-02635, RG342H, NARA*)

B-24L-1-CO 44-41428, which joined the 425th BS in November 1944, later became *The Big-Az-Burd*. Many natural metal Liberators had the lower fuselage and the underside of the wings painted black for night sea search missions. *The Big-Az-Burd* also eventually acquired a large sharksmouth too (*3A-01017, RG342H, NARA*)

increasing effort to flying supply missions within China to speed up the flow of supplies to outlying airfields. It completed 445 sorties between June and September, and then an additional 355 intra-China sorties in October and November. During these latter two months the 308th flew more supply sorties than it did combat missions, such was the demand for fuel and supplies. Routine as these missions might have been, they were not without cost. Between June and December nine B-24s were lost on flights over the 'Hump' or on supply missions within China.

During the last months of the year the 308th BG flew more sea search than bombing missions as attacks on shipping were deemed to be a more effective use of scarce gasoline than attacks on storage areas. The group had also been flying long range reconnaissance missions out into the South China Sea to locate Japanese shipping, passing the intelligence on to the US Navy for its carrier and submarine forces.

The 308th flew three bombing missions in October, six in November and six in December, the Japanese supply centre at Hankow remaining a priority target. Indeed, the group completed three night missions to Hankow during November and a fourth night mission in early December using pathfinders.

On 18 December 1944, in the biggest bombing mission the Fourteenth Air Force ever undertook, the 308th BG sent 30 aeroplanes to participate in a coordinated strike on Hankow with 84 B-29s from the Twentieth Air Force, 23 B-25s and a huge escort of Warhawks and Mustangs. The combined strike devastated the city.

ENDGAME IN CHINA

Although the 308th BG devoted most of its effort in January to attacking ships, there were fewer opportunities. The Fourteenth Air Force's unceasing attacks, the depredations of the US Navy's submarine force and the growing activities of American aeroplanes based in the Philippines resulted in a marked decline in the number of vessels sailing off the China coast. On many sea searches, the LAB B-24s ended up bombing secondary targets. A change in the overall military situation in China and a change in leadership dictated a new strategy. The Fourteenth Air Force shifted its priorities accordingly.

B-24L-1-CO 44-41427 *COCKY BOBBY* joined the 425th BS in the autumn of 1944. The bomber would fly some 39 missions and more than 50 flights over the 'Hump' during its time with the 308th BG (*Jim Augustus*)

In October 1944 Lt Gen Stilwell had been recalled to the United States, his place being taken as chief of staff to Generalissimo Chiang Kai-Shek and commander of all US forces in China by Lt Gen Albert Wedemeyer. The *Ichi-Go* operation concluded in December, although the Japanese Army pushed on to capture several of Chennault's remaining bases in eastern China during January. Wedemeyer decided to adopt a defensive strategy for several months in order to build up strength for a renewed offensive to begin in April 1945 with Chinese troops brought in from Burma. Additional Chinese divisions were also to be trained and armed by the Americans. Wedemeyer wanted Chennault and the Fourteenth Air Force to concentrate on destroying the JAAF in China and disrupting Japanese communications along the rail corridor from French Indochina to the north of the country.

With coastal shipping at a minimum, and the main ports and the Yangtze River frequently closed due to the 308th BG's repeated mining of these waters, the Japanese Army was now almost completely reliant on the railways. The Fourteenth Air Force was finally gaining the strength it needed to support a sustained campaign of rail interdiction. In the last few months of 1944 the Fourteenth Air Force began to receive more aircraft, more men and more supplies. While the pace of operations would always put a strain on the available reserves of fuel and other consumables, between October 1944 and January 1945 the Fourteenth Air Force's allocation of supplies flown over the 'Hump' nearly doubled. The 308th BG also received a steady flow of newer L- and M-model Liberators, bringing the group's total number of aircraft to 65+.

B-24L-1-CO 44-41429 *SETTIN' PRETTY* was the first L-model Liberator assigned to the 375th BS, the aircraft arriving in-theatre in October 1944 (*Jim Augustus*)

A formation of three B-24s from the 375th BS head for their target in early 1945 (*John V Osborne via the National Museum of the US Air Force*)

The rail system in north China became a priority target for the interdiction campaign, with the Fourteenth Air Force's medium bombers and fighters regularly shooting up locomotives and rolling stock. The Japanese would then take their damaged rail equipment to repair depots in northern China, and the latter, and adjacent rail yards, then became the main targets for the 308th BG.

In February the 308th BG moved three of its squadrons (the 374th, 375th and 425th) into the former Superfortress bases surrounding Chengtu, the B-29s having left for the Marianas. All the LAB bombers were transferred to the 373rd BS at this time, which remained at its base at Luliang to continue the sea search missions. The 375th BS also transferred several Liberators to the 373rd that had been used for radar reconnaissance/ferret missions, including B-24D 42-0635 *Spare Parts*, which must have been one of the last D-models to fly combat missions.

Five days after completing its move to the new bases, the group sent off 29 aeroplanes to bomb the rail yards at Shihchiachuang, only to find the target covered in cloud. It went back to the same target on 8 March with 34 aeroplanes, but due to haze and a Japanese smoke-screen the bombing was poor. The next day the 308th sent 32 B-24s to bomb the rail yards at Sinsiang, and better results were achieved. As one pilot recalled, 'navigation was excellent for China, and the run commenced as briefed. The target came up perfectly for the strike. We were credited with excellent results as 90 per cent of our bombs destroyed the target'.

Finally, on 16 March, another mission of 32 aeroplanes managed to hit the repair workshops at Shihchiachuang, getting 60 per cent of the bombs dropped in the target area. The attacks on rail yards in north China continued during the month, and as many of these targets had only minimal anti-aircraft defences so the bombers could make their runs at 10,000 ft, thus guaranteeing greater accuracy. These missions usually had an escort of P-51s, but by this time there was little risk of interception by Japanese fighters, which were being steadily withdrawn from China for defence of the homeland.

During March the 308th's squadrons bombed nine rail targets in north China and flew two missions against the main bridges over the Yellow River. On a mission to the rail yards at Kaifeng, 20 aircraft managed to drop 90 per cent of their ordnance directly onto a group of eight locomotives and 200 rail cars. Flying sea searches out of Luliang, the 373rd BS generated 108 sorties in March, claiming eight merchant vessels sunk totalling 26,550 tons. A destroyer and six more merchant vessels were probably sunk and another 11 damaged.

April brought the 308th BG's final bombing sorties of the war. In a mission against the rail repair yards at Taiyuan, the 308th had its last

The work of a remarkably talented artist, who also painted the nose art on B-24M *Stripped for Action*, B-24L-5-FO 44-49491 *Piece Time* gets the finishing touches before it receives its name. This aircraft was retired to the Walnut Ridge reclamation facility in Arkansas on 9 January 1946 (*Jim Augustus*)

encounter with a Japanese fighter. The group sent out 26 aeroplanes only to find clouds obscuring the target area. While circling to see if a hole would open up, an enemy fighter popped out of the clouds, avoided the P-51 escorts and made a frontal pass at one of the bombers, before diving back into the clouds to attack the same aeroplane from the rear, fortunately without effect.

The group flew several missions to attack Japanese storage areas and the Yellow River bridge, but its bombing role was coming to an end. Experience had shown that the medium bombers and the fighters were more efficient than the B-24s in the rail interdiction campaign, particularly the Mustangs with their long range and bomb-carrying capacity. The Liberators simply used up too much gasoline. The 308th flew its last group bombing mission on 19 April 1945 when 12 aircraft flying near the limit of the B-24's range bombed the rail repair facilities at Taiyuan, in northern China.

The 308th BG demolishes the rail yards at Kaifeng in March 1945 (*3A-02659, RG342H, NARA*)

The Fourteenth Air Force command decided to switch three of the 308th BG's four squadrons to 'hauling gas' over the 'Hump' for the medium bomber and fighter units, much to the disappointment of the crews involved. The 374th and 375th BSs duly began flying these missions from India to Chengtu in late April. Their B-24Js, Ls and Ms had their top and ball turrets removed, all guns and armament fixtures stripped from the nose and tail turrets, all armour plating dispensed with and three bomb-bay tanks installed. Crews were reduced to just the pilot, co-pilot, navigator, flight engineer and radio operator.

These 'Hump' missions cost the 374th BS its oldest aeroplane when B-24J *Ubangi Bag III* went missing on 8 May.

The 425th BS had a month's reprieve from 'hauling gas'. During April the squadron had received several aircraft equipped for Azon bombing, and it used them to successfully attack a number of key bridges in northern China during May. The 425th then converted to 'gas hauling'.

The 373rd BS continued to fly sea searches during April and May, but it was then decided to transfer the squadron to Okinawa so that its LAB-equipped bombers could participate in the air offensive against the Japanese homeland. This move was delayed until July, when the squadron flew to its new base at Yontan, on Okinawa, and joined the 494th BG. During June the remaining three squadrons transferred from China to a new base at Rupsi in Assam, India. For the next three-and-a-half months the 308th flew fuel from India to China, flying their last 'gas hauling' mission on 18 September, having completed 934 trips over the 'Hump'.

Some of the last bombing missions flown by the 308th BG were against bridges over the Yellow River (*John V Osborne via the National Museum of the US Air Force*)

Toward the end of the war the 308th BG's B-24s adopted elaborate nose art. The bomber's slab-sided fuselage formed a perfect canvas. B-24M-10-CO 44-42019 *CALAMITY JANE* served with the 374th BS (*Jim Augustus*)

The final configuration of *Miss Beryl*, with an impressive number of missions, 'Hump' flights and ships sunk painted on its fuselage. Converted into a tanker in March 1945, the aeroplane had the front turret removed and faired over so as to reduce weight (*Jim Augustus*)

On 5 May 1945, the second anniversary of the 308th BG's first combat mission, its CO, Col John Armstrong, issued a proclamation which aptly summed up the group's record in China;

'Saturday, 5 May marks the second anniversary of the first combat mission of the 308th BG. Our versatility as a heavy bombardment group has been proven by day and night attacks, high, medium and low-altitude bombing, mine laying and radar bombing. These sorties were against a variety of targets, most of which were heavily defended, in all kinds of weather and over poorly charted terrain. Units of this group have operated from behind enemy lines. Our men have become acclimated to enemy air raids and bombings, paucity of supplies and long periods of adverse weather conditions.

'In these two years, during which time the group has never exceeded 90 per cent of its authorised strength, we have flown 4039 combat sorties totalling 34,975 hours, flown 6486 ferrying sorties totalling 21,603 hours, shot down 222 enemy aeroplanes confirmed, dropped 4090 tons of bombs, laid 433 tons of mines, expended 481,000 rounds of ammunition, hauled 9827 tons of freight and supplies and sunk 185 enemy vessels totalling 678,000 tons. We have lost 116 aircraft and 53 crews, 164 men having been killed, 70 wounded and 312 posted as missing. A great many more have bailed out, but they have successfully walked back safely.

'This is only part of the story. No attempt is made here to describe the devotion to duty of the officers and men of this group or the heroism of the flyers whose deeds lie behind these statistics. In paying tribute to those men who have given their lives in order that the success we have achieved could be attained, we should resolve, as we enter our third year of tactical operations, to devote our energies and resources to one common goal – that of speeding in every way possible the final defeat of the enemy.'

The B-24's versatility made it invaluable for the changing conditions the Fourteenth Air Force faced in China. Whether flying conventional bombing missions, low-level attacks on shipping with the LAB system, or 'hauling gas' over the 'Hump', the B-24 proved its worth. For its operations in China the 308th BG received two Distinguished Unit Citations – one for its operations in China from May to August 1943, and a second for its sea search missions with the LAB system over the South China Sea, the Straits of Formosa and the Gulf of Tonkin from 24 May 1944 to 28 April 1945.

24th COMBAT MAPPING SQUADRON

There was one other unit that used the combat version of the B-24 in the China-Burma-India Theatre. The 24th Combat Mapping Squadron (CMS) flew the F-7, which was the reconnaissance version of the Liberator. Initially equipped with the basic F-7, it later added the improved F-7A and F-7B to its ranks as well. These aircraft carried trimetrogon and mosaic cameras in the nose and the aft bomb-bay.

Activated on 2 September 1942, the squadron moved to India in December 1943. Here, it was attached to the Tenth Air Force, the 24th CMS later becoming part of the 8th Photographic Group. Commencing operations in March 1944, the 24th flew missions in support of both the Tenth and the Fourteenth Air Forces and the British 14th Army. The squadron had detachments based in India and China for months at a time, and as with the 308th BG, the 24th's detachments in China had to fly their own fuel and supplies over the 'Hump'. And also like their bomber group counterparts, the squadron regularly flew its F-7s at well-above the recommended maximum gross weight. In 1944 the 24th made 182 'Hump' crossings, losing six Liberators during the course of these often hazardous missions.

Built as B-24L-15-CO 44-41680, this aircraft was converted into an F-7B and issued to the 24th CMS in India in late 1944. Note the unit badge on the Liberator's fin (*Peter M Bowers Collection, Museum of Flight*)

As its designation implies, the primary role of the 24th CMS was to reconnoitre large areas of territory and provide photographs directly to US Army or USAAF intelligence or to the Army's Map Service, who would then use the mosaics the squadron took to develop detailed maps of an area.

Flying separately or in small formations, the F-7s flew deep into enemy territory to gather their imagery. During the battle of Imphal, for example, the squadron made extensive mosaics of the Imphal-Kohima battle area to enable the 14th Army and the RAF to pinpoint Japanese targets. Later, the squadron produced mosaics of most of northern and central Burma for the 14th Army and for Stilwell's Chinese forces advancing on Myitkyina. It also provided extensive coverage of Thailand and the northern Malaya peninsula, with some of these missions involving flights of 2500 miles or more.

More mundane, but no less invaluable, was a mission to provide the ATC with photography of a 50-mile wide strip of the route from Calcutta to Kunming, as well as key airfields in India. This imagery was then used to aid ATC pilots flying the 'Hump' route.

From July 1944 until February 1945 the squadron operated out of China. As the navigators of the 308th BG found to their frustration, large areas of China were poorly mapped, if at all. Concentrating on Japanese-occupied territory, during its period in China the 24th provided extensive photographic coverage of the China coast from Shanghai to French Indochina, as well as coverage of large areas in central China where the *Ichi-Go* operation was underway. The unit received a special commendation from Maj Gen Stratemeyer for these successful missions.

In total the 24th CMS covered some 455,000 square miles of territory in India, Burma, Thailand and Malaya, and 435,000 square miles in China. From March 1944 through to February 1945, the squadron produced 242,050 prints for other units in China and Burma. Weather proved to be the most difficult challenge on these missions, for roughly half of all aborted sorties were due to poor conditions. Remarkably, these individual reconnaissance flights were hardly ever challenged, although the F-7s usually flew with all guns manned and armed. In December 1945 the 24th CMS moved to the Philippines, where the unit continued its photographic mapping missions across Asia until June 1946.

APPENDICES

B-24 UNITS OF THE CBI

TENTH AIR FORCE

7th Bombardment Group

Commanders
Col Conrad F Necrason (1 July 1942 to 27 March 1944)
Col Aubrey K Dodson (27 March to 6 November 1944)
Col Harvey T Alness (6 November 1944 to 25 June 1945)
Col Howard F Bronson (25 June 1945 to end of war)

Squadrons
9th, 436th (formerly 88th BS), 492nd and 493rd

24th Combat Mapping Squadron

FOURTEENTH AIR FORCE

308th Bombardment Group

Commanders
Col Eugene H Beebe (16 September 1942 to 3 November 1943)
Col William P Fisher (3 November 1943 to 19 October 1944)
Col John G Armstrong (19 October 1944 to 1 July 1945)
Col William D Hopson (1 July 1945 to end of war)

Squadrons
373rd, 374th, 375th and 425th

COLOUR PLATES

1
B-24J-30-CO 42-73303 *FROZEN/"HOT" TO GO* of the 9th BS/7th BG, Pandaveswar, India, mid-1944
Originally named simply *"HOT TO GO"*, this Consolidated-built aeroplane was one of the early J-model Liberators assigned to the 9th BS in October 1943. Camouflaged in the standard olive drab and neutral grey scheme of the period, *FROZEN/"HOT" TO GO* became a popular backdrop for photographs, with hands placed on the appropriate part of the woman's anatomy. In its long service with the unit 42-73303 flew 60+ bombing missions and 37 arduous 'Hump' flights.

2
B-24J-185-CO 44-40857 *RANGOON RANGLER* of the 9th BS/7th BG, Pandaveswar, India, late 1944
RANGOON RANGLER was a late model B-24J which was accepted by the USAAF on 23 May 1944 and sent overseas a month later. The aeroplane carried the 9th BS's black and white chequered tail markings. The cowgirl on the nose was copied from the famous Alberto Vargas painting of March 1944. The port side of this aeroplane carried artwork of a cowboy with the name *Cactus Kid*. *RANGOON RANGLER/Cactus Kid* flew at least 51 bombing missions, 31 'Hump' sorties and claimed a Japanese aircraft destroyed. At the end of the war the B-24 was flown back to the US and turned over to the Reconstruction Finance Corporation (RFC) for scrapping.

3
B-24J-190-CO 44-40985 *SHY ANN* of the 9th BS/ 7th BG, Pandaveswar, India, late 1944
A San Diego-built late model B-24J, this aircraft was named *SHY ANN* in a play on the city of Cheyenne, Wyoming. The aeroplane was delivered to the USAAF on 10 June 1944 and departed the US on 2 September. *SHY ANN* was marked up with the white and black chequered rudder and horizontal yellow stripe markings that the 9th BS adopted during 1944. 44-40985 did not enjoy a long career with the 9th. Assigned to a special 7th BG composite squadron tasked with flying supplies and gasoline to isolated Fourteenth Air Force bases in China, it crashed on 18 December 1944 shortly after taking off from the airfield at Luliang. The bomber was being flown by the 436th BS crew led by Lt Joseph Richards at the time, and they all perished in the accident.

4
B-24M-15-FO 44-50857 *HOME STRETCH* of the 436th BS/7th BG, Madhaiganj, India, April 1945
At the end of 1944 L- and M-model Liberators began to progressively replace the 7th BG's B-24Js. Built at the Ford Willow Run plant in January 1945, 44-50857 was sent overseas on 7 March. Retaining its natural metal finish, *HOME STRETCH* carries the yellow and black chequered upper tail markings of the 436th BS and the suggestive nose art. The B-24 returned to the US at war's end and joined thousands of other aircraft waiting to be scrapped at Kingman, Arizona.

5
B-24M-25-CO 44-42251 *"Slower Than Rotation"* of the 436th BS/7th BG, Madhaiganj, India, spring 1945
"Slower Than Rotation" was a Consolidated San Diego-built B-24M delivered to the USAAF on 10 February 1945. Assigned to the 436th BS, it was marked with aeroplane No 62, and later No 75. The bomber's name was likely a humorous comment on the speed of the B-24 in relation to the speed of personnel rotation from India back home at the end of a combat tour, which to some seemed to take forever. Like many of its sisters, 44-42251 returned to the US in late 1945 for disposal through the RFC at Walnut Ridge, Arkansas.

6
B-24J-15-CO 42-73160 *JUNGLE JIG* of the 492nd BS/7th BG, Madhaiganj, India, late 1944
Accepted on 24 September 1943, *JUNGLE JIG* was one of the first B-24Js assigned to the 7th BG, arriving in India on 1 November 1943. It was also one of the longest serving. In 1944 *JUNGLE JIG* was adorned with the white and black chequered upper fin markings newly allocated to the 492nd BS. By May 1945 *JUNGLE JIG* had flown 84 combat missions and 35 trips over the 'Hump', hauling 60,000 gallons of fuel to China. 42-73160 flew on every type of mission, from high altitude bombing to low-level attacks on bridges and strafing locomotives and rolling stock, claiming two aircraft shot down and one bridge destroyed. In the process, the aeroplane accumulated 1470.50 hours of flying time and went through three complete sets of Pratt & Whitney R-1830 engines. The aeroplane was still with the squadron, flying second line duties, in July 1945. It returned to the United States for disposal in November 1945, ending up at Walnut Ridge, Arkansas.

7
B-24J-200-CO 44-41222 *Lovable Lorena* of the 492nd BS/7th BG, Madhaiganj, India, late 1944
A late model B-24J built at Consolidated's San Diego plant, *Lovable Lorena* was delivered to the USAAF on 31 August 1944 and left for overseas duty on 26 September. Upon its arrival in India, the aeroplane was assigned to the 492nd BS at Madhaiganj, and it was marked up with the squadron's white and black chequers on the upper fin section. *Lovable Lorena* flew more than 30 combat missions, and in June 1945 switched to hauling gasoline over the 'Hump' with the rest of the squadron. *Lovable Lorena* was lost with its crew in a crash during just such a mission on the night of 28 July 1945.

8

B-24D-10-CO 41-23921 *"Sittin' Bull"* of the 493rd BS/7th BG, Pandaveswar, India, late 1943

"Sittin' Bull" was one of the first B-24Ds assigned to the 493rd BS, the bomber taking part in the squadron's inaugural combat mission on 26 January 1943. At that time the 7th BG's practice was to paint over the aeroplane's serial number on the tail, leaving only the individual plane number in black. During the course of the next nine months *"Sittin' Bull"* flew an additional 55 missions. With the arrival of B-24Js in October 1943 to replace the D-models, the USAAF decided to bring back a veteran combat aeroplane from the CBI Theatre to undertake a war bond tour of the United States. *"Sittin' Bull"* was chosen to be that aeroplane, and it was duly re-named *RANGOON RAMBLER*. With a crew made up of combat veterans under the leadership of Capt Raymond C Rote, the aeroplane flew back to the United States in November 1943. *RANGOON RAMBLER* featured in a USAAF recruiting advertisement describing a mission over Burma, with a painting depicting the bomber flying over the Rangoon docks, although it never actually flew a combat mission with that name. The aeroplane was unceremoniously scrapped post-war.

9

B-24D-25-CO 41-24302 *BOISTEROUS BITCH* of the 493rd BS/7th BG, Pandaveswar, India, September-October 1943

This San Diego-built B-24D arrived in India in April 1943 and was assigned to the 493rd BS. Named *BOISTEROUS BITCH*, the aeroplane flew during the monsoon season when weather conditions obscured targets and caused the cancellation of many missions. As with a number of other B-24Ds in the group at this time, *BOISTEROUS BITCH* lacked the Sperry ball turret. Indeed, the 493rd BS did not receive a D-model Liberator with a ball turret until August 1943. *BOISTEROUS BITCH* left the squadron on 8 November 1943 to make way for the newer B-24Js. It was apparently condemned overseas in November 1944.

10

B-24J-15-CO 42-73158 *PECKER RED* of the 493rd BS/7th BG, Madhaiganj, India, early 1945

PECKER RED was one of the first B-24Js assigned to the 493rd BS. Initially given plane No 60, it survived the intense air battles that took place during November and December of 1943, the bomber's gunners claiming eight Japanese fighters destroyed. In 1944 the yellow and black chequered rudder marking designating the 493rd BS was added to the aeroplane. Later in the year *PECKER RED* was re-numbered 67. By January 1945 42-73158 was the oldest aeroplane in the 493rd, having completed at least 89 combat missions. On 28 January 1945, while returning from a supply mission to China, the aircraft's No 2 engine had to be shut down and the pilot made a precautionary landing at Imphal. By now there was a steady flow

of L- and M-model Liberators reaching India, so the 7th BG decided to simply leave *PECKER RED* at Imphal – a sad end for such a gallant old warhorse.

11

B-24J-190-CO 44-40989 *Double Trouble* of the 493rd BS/7th BG, Madhaiganj, India, March 1945

This late-model B-24J was delivered to the USAAF on 14 June 1944, and after modification departed the United States for overseas service on 2 September. Assigned to the CBI Theatre, *Double Trouble* was one of ten B-24Js from the 493rd BS modified to carry the Azon radio-controlled bomb. The natural metal aircraft boasts the yellow and black chequers of the 493rd BS on its rudder. Note the three antennas under the tail turret for the Azon bomb gear. In March 1945, with Japanese air opposition now negligible, the 493rd BS removed all the Sperry ball turrets from its Liberators. The aeroplane returned to the US at the end of 1945 fordisposal at Walnut Ridge.

12

B-24M-20-FO 44-51054 *FLAME OF THE SQUADRON* of the 493rd BS/7th BG, Madhaiganj, India, July 1945

FLAME OF THE SQUADRON was a Ford-built B-24M delivered to the USAAF on 9 March 1945. The aeroplane left the United States on 3 May 1945, and after arrival in India it was assigned to the 493rd BS. With the liberation of Burma and the end of the Strategic Air Force the missions of the 493rd BS shifted to raids on airfields in Thailand and dropping propaganda leaflets over Thai towns and cities by day and by night. The 493rd camouflaged a number of the B-24Ms assigned to the unit with a high gloss black paint that was considered to provide better protection against searchlights. 44-51054 shows the standard application of the high gloss black on the underside of the wings, the rudder and on the fuselage. The inspiration for the nose art was an Alberto Vargas calendar from January 1945. Following the cessation of hostilities in the CBI the bomber was condemned and salvaged for parts.

13

B-24D-25-CO 41-24223 *DOODLEBUG* of the 373rd BS/308th BG, Yangkai, China, October-November 1943

A San Diego-built D-model, *DOODLEBUG* was one of the original nine B-24Ds assigned to the 373rd BS. Lt Bernard O'Hara and his crew flew the aeroplane to China, leaving the United States on 15 February 1943 with the rest of the 308th BG. At the Tenth Air Force air depot at Agra, in India, a number of the 308th BG's B-24Ds, possibly including *DOODLEBUG*, had nose art painted on them by a Cpl A C Mitchell, who was stationed at the depot. In the first version of *DOODLEBUG*'s nose art the comely young lady sat naked on the bomb – a bathing suit was added later. The aircraft's mission list provides a graphic illustration of the logistical problems that confronted the 308th BG in China.

During the bomber's ten months in-theatre, *DOODLEBUG* and its crews flew 11 bombing missions and more than 50 sorties over the 'Hump' ferrying gasoline, bombs and other supplies for the 308th. The aircraft's gunners claimed ten Japanese fighters shot down and 18 probably destroyed in a running battle lasting 25 minutes during the disastrous mission to Haiphong on 15 September 1943 when a large group of fighters attacked the small 373rd BS formation. SSgt Charles E Edwards and TSgt Joseph E Murray both claimed three fighters destroyed and five probables. JAAF aircraft downed three of the five 373rd B-24s attacking Haiphong and damaged a fourth so badly that it crashed on landing back at Kunming. *DOODLEBUG* was the only bomber to return safely to Yangkai. It was sent home in December 1943 in company with fellow 308th BG veterans *THE MIGHTY EIGHTBALL*, *The Pelican* and *Snowball From Hell*.

14

B-24J-30-CO 42-73286 *Esky* of the 373rd BS/ 308th BG, Luliang, China, late 1944
Esky was built at Consolidated's San Diego plant and delivered on 16 October 1943. The aeroplane was named for *Esquire* magazine's mascot, a mustachioed figure often depicted chasing young women, shown in this case running after a comely young Chinese lady. *Esquire* was a popular men's magazine of the day which featured the pin-up paintings of Alberto Vargas, a source of inspiration for many aircraft nose art designs. In early 1944 the squadrons of the 308th BG began to add coloured tail markings to their aircraft, the 373rd BS painting the rudders of its aircraft red. Later in the year the group added large sharksmouths to its B-24s. *Esky* was salvaged in July 1945.

15

B-24D-20-CO 41-24183 *The GOON* of the 374th BS/308th BG, Chengkung, China, early 1944
One of the original group of B-24s that flew to China in February 1943 when the 308th BG was transferred to the CBI Theatre, *The GOON* was a San Diego-built B-24D named after a character in the *Popeye* cartoon strip. *The GOON* became famous as the mount of TSgt Arthur P Benko, who, as its top turret gunner, was credited with 16 Japanese fighters shot down in combat, three probables and one damaged. At 32, Benko was older than most of his crewmates. Growing up in Arizona, he had been an avid hunter and marksman. Indeed, before the war Benko was a state rifle and skeet champion. After gunnery training he joined the 308th BG and flew overseas with his crew in *The GOON*. Benko claimed five fighters destroyed and one damaged on the rugged 21 August 1943 mission to Hankow, but his best day came on the 1 October 1943 mission to Haiphong when, in a running battle lasting 40 minutes, he claimed seven Japanese fighters shot down. Benko's guns jammed twice during the fight. 'I never worked that turret so fast before', he told a reporter after his return. 'They tell me the scrap lasted 40 minutes, but it seemed like a minute to me. You have to be on the alert every second'. His feat made national news back in the United States, Benko attributing his success partly to luck and partly to his practice of what he called 'ink shooting' – throwing a tin can or an egg up in the air and shooting it without using the gunsights, which taught him how to hit a moving target. In early December, returning from a night mission to bomb the docks in Kowloon, *The GOON* lost power in two engines. 1Lt Samuel Skousen ordered the crew to bail out, and Benko and bombardier Lt Malcom Sanders landed in Japanese-held territory and were captured. They were both later executed. Ironically, Skousen managed to fly *The GOON* back to Chengkung on the remaining two engines. In early 1944 the bomber had the yellow rudder and yellow triangle marking applied to its tail, denoting the 374th BS.

16

B-24D-165-CO 42-40503 *"JUNGLE PUSSY"* of the 374th BS/308th BG, Chengkung, China, summer 1944
42-40503 was a late-model B-24D built at the Consolidated-Vultee plant in San Diego in March 1943. The aeroplane was modified at the Oklahoma City Modification Center to take a Consolidated gun turret in the nose and an enlarged lower nose section to provide adequate visibility for the bombardier. Sent to Langley, Virginia, 42-40503 was fitted with the Low Altitude Bombing (LAB) system for low altitude, radar-guided attacks on enemy shipping. So-called 'snooper' Liberators with this modification were sometimes referred to unofficially as 'SB-24s'. The dramatic nose art worn by this aircraft was applied before the bomber departed for overseas service in May 1944. The aeroplane had been intended for the FEAF, which had begun receiving 'snooper' B-24s in the autumn of 1943, but it was sent to the 308th BG instead to augment the Fourteenth Air Force's small LAB bomber force. Assigned to the 374th BS, it was named *"JUNGLE PUSSY"*. The aeroplane carried the 374th's yellow rudder squadron marking, but contemporary photographs do not show the yellow triangle on the tail normally associated with B-24s ftom this unit.

17

B-24J-205-CO 44-41294 *TAYLOR MAID* of the 374th BS/308th BG, Chengkung, China, summer 1945
TAYLOR MAID was a late model B-24J equipped with the LAB system that was delivered on 2 September 1944 and sent overseas 18 days later. Assigned to the 374th BS, the aeroplane featured the squadron's yellow rudder and triangle markings on the tail, a sharksmouth on the nose and matt black undersurfaces for night sea sweeps. The B-24's slab-sided fuselage made an excellent canvas for nose art. Toward the end of the war the 308th BG boasted some highly creative

and wonderfully expressive artwork on its bombers. The aeroplane's name, *TAYLOR MAID*, was a play on words, with the nose art being based on a 1939 Gil Elvgren pin-up titled 'French Dressing'. During its career with the 374th BS, *TAYLOR MAID* flew at least 48 combat missions and completed 44 flights over the 'Hump'. The aeroplane survived the war and was returned to the US at the end of 1945. Turned over to the RFC, it ended its days sitting with 1148 other surplus Liberators at Walnut Creek.

18

B-24M-15-CO 44-42133 *MISS LACE* of the 374th BS/308th BG, Chengkung, China, 1945

A Consolidated-built M-model delivered on 19 January 1945, *MISS LACE* was another example of the elaborate nose art that many of the 308th BG's B-24s featured toward the end of the war. Named after the famous character in Milton Caniff's wartime comic strip *Male Call*, *MISS LACE* featured the yellow rudder and tail triangle of the 374th BS, a sharksmouth on the nose and matt black undersurfaces for night sea sweeps. The aeroplane flew 34 combat missions and claimed two ships sunk. When the 308th BG ceased bombing missions in the summer of 1945, *MISS LACE* had its armament removed and was transferred with other group B-24s to hauling fuel over the 'Hump' in bomb-bay tanks. The bomber returned home at the end of 1945 for disposal through the RFC.

19

B-24J-45-CO 42-73445 *GEORGIA PEACH* of the 375th BS/308th BG, Chengkung, China, late 1944

GEORGIA PEACH was delivered to the USAAF's Tucson Modification Center on 27 October 1943, but spent some time in the United States before going overseas in December of that year. Assigned to the 375th BS, the aeroplane acquired the unit's black-white-black rudder stripes in early 1944, adding a sharksmouth in the latter half of the year. The bomber appears to have retained its olive drab and neutral grey camouflage throughout its time in the frontline. The nose art was based on an Alberto Vargas pin-up from December 1943. *GEORGIA PEACH* flew at least 36 combat missions and was finally withdrawn from service in March 1945. It managed to survive the war, returning to the US and ending up at Walnut Creek with its sister ship *TAYLOR MAID*.

20

B-24J-175-CO 44-40584 *KING'S "X"* of the 375th BS/308th BG, Chengkung, China, late 1944

KING'S "X" was a late-build J-model from the last production run completed by Consolidated. The aeroplane was delivered in April 1944 and flown directly to China, where it was assigned to the 375th BS. Many natural metal Liberators had the underside of their wings and fuselage painted in matt black for night missions. In addition to the black-white-black rudder markings of the 375th, *KING'S "X"* had a sharksmouth painted on later in the year. The name and nose art were taken from the popular comic strip, *The Little King*. Returning from a mission to bomb the Shihchiachuang rail yards on 23 February 1945, *KING'S "X"* was badly damaged when its nose gear collapsed on landing. The bomber was duly scrapped in China.

21

B-24D-25-CO 41-24293 *"SHERAZADE"* of the 425th BS/308th BG, Kunming, China, late 1943

"SHERAZADE", named after the heroine of the popular 1942 film *Arabian Nights*, was one of the original B-24Ds the 308th BG brought to China in February 1943. The aeroplane illustrates the basic camouflage and markings of the group's D-models during 1943, which consisted of the standard olive drab and neutral grey colours, national insignia, with the bomber's serial number and plane number in yellow on the tail. On 24 August 1943, *"SHERAZADE"* was the lead ship in a formation of seven B-24s from the 425th BS sent to bomb Hankow. Maj Horace Foster was the pilot and Lt Donald Kohsiek the co-pilot on the mission. The attacking 'Oscars' from the 25th and 33rd Sentais made repeated passes against the formation, shooting down four B-24s. At the end of 40 minutes of attacks that had damaged the aeroplane's bomb-bay, right wing and fuselage, an 'Oscar' made a last pass at *"SHERAZADE"*, sending a stream of 12.7 mm shells down the length of the fuselage. One of the first rounds entered the cockpit and exploded directly in front of Maj Foster's head, killing him instantly. Kohsiek was momentarily stunned after receiving a face full of plexiglas and shell fragments. Lt Morton Salk, the bombardier, came up from the nose to remove Foster from the pilot's seat and then flew the aircraft until Kohsiek could resume command. That day a Chinese officer was flying with the crew as a third pilot, and he took over from Salk in helping Kohsiek fly the battered aeroplane, which was leaking oil and fuel, back to the USAAF airfield at Hengyang. Kohsiek duly landed without brakes. *"SHERAZADE"* was repaired and flown back to Kunming, only to be destroyed in a crash-landing on 25 January 1944 at Chabua, in India, after completing a flight over the 'Hump'.

22

B-24L-1-CO 44-41427 *COCKY BOBBY* of the 425th BS/308th BG, Kunming, summer 1945

COCKY BOBBY was one of 417 B-24Ls built at the Consolidated San Diego factory. Delivered on 11 September 1944, the aeroplane was sent overseas ten days later. When the bomber arrived in China it was initially assigned to the 373rd BS, but the aircraft was later transferred to the 425th BS. The Liberator was soon marked with the latter unit's yellow and black stripes on the rudder and a sharksmouth on the nose. On the 425th's later natural metal finish J-, L- and M-models, the unit employed a simpler rudder marking consisting of fewer yellow and black stripes than it had used on earlier olive drab/neutral grey Liberators. *COCKY*

BOBBY flew its first few missions in its natural metal finish, but the aircraft subsequently had matt black paint applied to the undersurfaces of the wings and fuselage for night missions. By the summer of 1945 *COCKY BOBBY* had completed 39 combat missions and at least 50 'Hump' flights, indicated by the large camel figure next to the nose art. The B-24 survived the war and was sent home for disposal at the end of 1945.

23

B-25M-30-FO 44-51508 *Stripped for ACTION* of the 425th BS/308th BG, India, October 1945

A Ford-built M-model, *Stripped for ACTION* left the Willow Run plant on 11 April 1945, and was delivered to a USAAF modification center at St Paul, Minnesota, 48 hours later. The aeroplane departed the US on 21 May, arriving in China a few weeks later. Once in-theatre the aeroplane was given a coat of high gloss black paint on the underside of its wings and on the fuselage sides up to the wings, similar in pattern to late model B-24s serving with the 7th BG. By this time the 308th BG had ceased combat missions and was spending most of its time flying supply missions over the 'Hump' hauling fuel for fighters and medium bombers in China. *Stripped for ACTION* had one of the racier examples of nose art in the 308th BG, being another gem painted by David Attie. He also applied the nose art for *Piece Time*, although this apparently did not win the approval of the commanding officer at the time. Attie again used a Gil Elvgren pin-up as his inspiration – in this case Elvgren's 'Weight Control', which showed a buxom young woman on her back using a weight machine. Attie went one better than Elvgren, removing the young lady's brassiere from the original pin-up to reveal all of her considerable charms. *Stripped for ACTION* appears to have remained in the Far East for some time after the end of the war, finally returning home in January 1947 and being condemned for salvage.

24

F-7A 42-73038 *Rice Pattie Hattie* of the 24th CMS/ 8th RG, Cox's Bazar, India, February-April 1945

The 24th CMS flew a mix of natural metal finished F-7As and aircraft painted in the special Synthetic Haze paint scheme. The latter consisted of two colours, with the aeroplane initially being painted deep sky blue overall and then a special white enamel, tinted a very pale blue, being sprayed on the fuselage sides and in areas of shadow under the wings and horizontal tail. The Synthetic Haze scheme did not stand up well to the rigours of the climate in the CBI, leading to a patchy appearance as shown here on *Rice Pattie Hattie*. Apart from the name and nose art, based on an Alberto Vargas pin-up from September 1943, the F-7A carried the emblem of the 24th CMS on the tail. This aeroplane was a B-24J-5-CO accepted on 2 September 1943 and sent to St Paul, Minnesota, for modification into an F-7A. It returned to the US in November 1945 for disposal.

INDEX

References to illustrations are shown in **bold**. Plates are shown with page and caption locators in brackets.